PRAISE FOR *WISE PARENTING: CREATING THE JOY OF FAMILY*

Dr. Gil Stieglitz is the real deal. His faith, leadership and writings have never wavered over the fifteen years I've known him. I love the intentionality, wisdom, and practicality Gil brings to parenting in his book *Wise Parenting*. Every parent should read it to gain solid understanding and practical ways to guide their children.

—Jay Stearley, Pastor and Missionary, Slingshot Consultant, former Executive Pastor, Author of *Begin*.

I have known Gil for over 20 years as a leader, pastor, and loyal friend. Most of all, I have observed his priorities—God, family, and church. In his newest book *Wise Parenting*, he shares decades of being "Dad." This book demonstrates his life-long quest to be a great parent, and will be an immense help for those on that same journey.

—Conrad Lowe, Pastor, Denominational Leader, Executive Coach, and Mentor

Dr. Gil's *Wise Parenting* book is truly full of practical family wisdom that will help you have a healthier family. Gil has tested out his theories with families for several decades. His gift at storytelling is invaluable in unpacking these valuable family principles. Your money will be well spent on this new family book.

—Rev. Dr. Ed Hird, co-author of *Blue Sky*, a novel about family reconciliation.

We may have missed a conversation with Solomon or what Christ shared on the Emmaus road, but we can glean from decades of research, parenting, and pastoring from my longtime friends Drs. Gil and Dana Stieglitz as they share key principles of successful parenting. This book, *Wise Parenting*, is filled with proven principles that read like an engaging informal conversation. Implementing these principles, which will require planning and work, will bring greater joy to your family. If for you there is no greater joy than to see your children mature into successful individuals, *Wise Parenting* is a rewarding read.

—Dr. Ken Townsend, Head of Schools Grace Cascade Christian Schools, former ACSI NW Regional Director

"Gil and Dana Stieglitz are trusted guides in life. Their most recent book, *Wise Parenting*, provides a road map for your journey. If you are a new parent, devour it! If you are an experienced (and bruised!) parent, drink it in and receive healing and hope. I once wrote that we all need to be "re-parented" at some point in our lives. Whether you are a first time parent, an adult in need of re-parenting, or an experienced parent, this book gives you practical wisdom and timeless truth for your journey."

—Dr. John Jackson, President of William Jessup University, Author & Speaker

"These materials made all the difference in our home. Thank you for introducing all the techniques, ideas, and plans. We needed almost all of them."

—Wise Parenting class attendee

"I was at the end of my rope with my ten-year old, and then I talked with Dr. Gil about what to do. I tried what he suggested and it was like magic; she behaved and our relationship is on the mend. Thank you."

—Wise Parenting mentee

W!SE PARENTING

Creating the Joy of Family

BY

DR. GIL STIEGLITZ
DR. DANA STIEGLITZ

Wise Parenting: Creating the Joy of Family
Copyright © 2020 by Drs. Gil and Dana Stieglitz

Published by Principles to Live By, P.O. Box 214, Roseville CA 95661.
For more information about this book and the authors, visit www.ptlb.com.

Copyedited by:
Jennifer Edwards
jedwardsediting.net

Cover Design by:
Dave Eaton

Book Design & Typography by:
Linné Garrett
829Design.com

Print: 978-0-9968855-9-1
E-book: 978-0-9909640-9-4
Audiobook: 978-1-952736-00-1

All rights reserved. No part of this publication may be reproduced, stored in a retrieval system, or transmitted in any way by any means—electronic, mechanical, photocopy, recording, or otherwise—without the prior permission of the copyright holder, except as provided by USA copyright law. When reproducing text from this book, include the following credit line: "*Wise Parenting: Creating the Joy of Family* by Drs. Gil and Dana Stieglitz, published by Principles to Live By Publishing. Used by permission."

Unless otherwise indicated, all Scripture quotations are taken from the NEW AMERICAN STANDARD BIBLE®, Copyright © 1960, 1962, 1963, 1968, 1971, 1972, 1973, 1975, 1977, 1995 by The Lockman Foundation. Used by permission.

Scripture quotations marked NIV are taken from THE HOLY BIBLE, NEW INTERNATIONAL VERSION®, NIV® Copyright © 1973, 1978, 1984, 2011 by Biblica, Inc.® Used by permission. All rights reserved worldwide.

Scripture quotations marked NLT are taken from the *Holy Bible*, New Living Translation, copyright © 1996, 2004, 2015 by Tyndale House Foundation. Used by permission of Tyndale House Publishers, Inc., Carol Stream, Illinois 60188. All rights reserved.

Scripture quotations marked KJV are taken from The King James Version as present on Bible Gateway matching the 1987 printing. The KJV is public domain in the United States.

PRINTED IN THE UNITED STATES OF AMERICA

✤ Dedication ✤

This book is dedicated to
Jenessa, Abbey, and Grace Stieglitz,
our three daughters who so greatly increase our joy.

Contents

On Your Way to the Family You've Always Wanted 11

The Six R's of Wise Parenting

    1 Relationship 23

    2 Respect 41

    3 Resources 55

    4 Rules 67

    5 Routines 91

    6 Responsibility 109

Final Thoughts 135

Notes 139

Appendices

    1 Personality Tests and Other Resources 141

    2 Sample Placemats of Ten Commandments and Other Key Scriptures 145

    3 The Box Illustration 147

    4 Consequences: Words (Reproof) & Actions (Rod) 149

    5 Wise Parenting Slides 151

    6 Six R's of Wise Parenting Table 153

About Gil & Dana Stieglitz and Principles to Live By 155

More PTLB Resources 156

On Your Way to the Family You've Always Wanted

Years ago, I got a call to go to the local jail to visit a young man I knew very well. As I listened to him tell his story, I struggled to understand how Jim, Mark's son, could be in jail for trying to murder someone. Jim's father and mother were some of the most upstanding people I had ever known. I remember thinking that parenting really does need an instruction manual. His parents had made only one mistake that I could discern, but then some mistakes in parenting can change everything. Jim's life, his parents, and their family would never be the same because of what he had done. Strangely enough, it was Jim's story and my deep understanding of his family which allowed me to put together this work—a compilation of *the* six parenting essentials every parent should know, which I affectionately call "wise parenting."

As a pastor, I have seen just about everything there is to see, and I've heard every type of story about individuals and families. I spent seventeen years working in a forgotten corner of Los Angeles County, where wonderful people did the best they could to raise their children amidst meth dealers, gangs, poverty, guns, insane commutes, and every kind of temptation imaginable. I can recount many, many families who were destroyed by the teenager who got sucked into gangs; the mother who started stepping out on her husband; the screaming, yelling, and fighting of a family member; or the parent who had just stopped caring or coming home altogether. One thing I learned: families may face their own version of tragedy every day, but *all* families suffer.

In the beginning of my work with parents and teens, I could not see any patterns explaining why one family did well and another came unglued. It didn't seem to be how much money the parents made. It wasn't whether the family went to church (much to my discouragement). It wasn't how well the kids did in school. In fact, some people were telling me there weren't any discernable patterns at all; it was random and could happen to anyone. But eventually, I did begin to see a simple pattern emerge for each family who did it right and an absence of that pattern in families who came apart. I want to share with you this simple pattern that I know works.

As a pastor who cares deeply about healthy relationships, my job is to give parents *hope* that their families *can* be enjoyable places where their kids will find love, nurturing, and energy so they can grow up to be great people. We want kids who will make a difference in their world and love God and the people in their life. We want successful, joy-filled families whose members want to be together and each one is thriving, contributing, and valued. This is the goal.

To get there, we need to implement six essential elements, each one a crucial "ingredient," if you will. The six ingredients make up the pattern I see in successful families, and are things you may already know about, for they have been called by many names: love, value, resources, expectations, habits, and responsibility. When blended together, they create the wonderful dynamic we call "family." Trust me when I say that when these six elements are present relationally, they do wonderful things:

*They make the members of any group of people
feel delighted to be a part of it.*

*They make each member proud to be a part of that family—
that they are viable and valued.*

*They allow for the family to produce far more than
any of the individuals could alone.*

This is how family should be.

The Six R's

For the purposes of this book and ease of remembering them, I will introduce these ingredients as the Six R's. There is significant overlap between these elements, but they are distinct. This is the way I think about them:

LOVE

Relationship **R**espect **R**esources
(love) *(value)* *(money & mentoring)*

TRAINING

Rules **R**outines **R**esponsibility
(expectations) *(habits)* *(correction)*

I've been teaching and training parents on the "Six R's of Wise Parenting" for over thirty years now, and I recently saw a new pattern emerge from these principles. The first three R's have to do with *loving* our children and our family. These are Relationship, Respect, and Resources. If we truly *love* our children, we will make sure that we are vitally connected to them in loving *relationships*. We will also treat them with *respect and value* and help them learn to respect us and the important things around them. And we will *resource or provide* our children with what they need in terms of wisdom, mentors and guides, as well as financially, emotionally, mentally, spiritually, relationally, and physically. These first three R's demonstrate to our children that we love them. Their absence says the opposite. How can you really love someone if you never spend time with them… if you demean them…or you don't provide the mentors and resources they need to thrive? These three R's are powerful.

But it is not enough to fill our children up with love, so we must also *train* them or else the joy of being together will not emerge. Children have to be taught how to successfully live in our presence and in the presence of others. These next three R's are about *training*—Rules, Routines, and Responsibility. For a family to have joy, we all must understand the *rules and expectations* of the house. As parents, we are the makers and keepers of the rules, so we will have to say them thousands of times until they are crystal clear to everyone. We will also have to learn and practice *key routines* until they are a part of the way we operate. No one wants to be in a group where one person gets to do whatever they want while others have to help make the family work. Lastly, there will need to be ways of talking about what didn't work. Each person will have to take *responsibility* for when they didn't do something they should have, when they did something they shouldn't, and when they did something really damaging to the family. We have to have corrective conversations, which must have the ability to bring about change in the child's behaviors, words, and attitudes. Without corrective change the joy of family is impossible.

Let's just be honest...biology does not mean that the joy of family will emerge. Just because a family is related does not mean that the family will like being together or accomplish anything significant. It takes all six of these R's to create the joy that everyone is looking for, where each member wants to be a part of their particular family. When parents and children do not participate in the implementation of Relationship, Respect, Resources, Rules, Routine, and Responsibility, then the typical family is just a board and care house. If, on the other hand, these elements are constantly injected into a family, then the children and the parents want to be together, and they form a loving group that pulls for one another and the joy emerges.

Personally, I work hard to add each one into every group I'm a part of, especially my marriage and family. God wants to partner with us to create dynamic groups (family) everywhere we go, so I also add the Six R's to my work relationships, inject them into my small group at church, and pour them into the mix of my wife, kids, and friendships.

Yes, you can also form a "family" within any team or group you are a part of. If any of these relational units are added in, then the wonder—the spirit and sense of "family" will begin to emerge there too. If any are missing, "family" will either not be created at all or what was there will be eroded or destroyed.

We've all seen families where these elements weren't present, and the individuals couldn't wait to get away from the "family." We may have also seen or been a part of a business, church, or team where these ingredients are functioning, and we witness significantly different individuals who can't seem to get enough time together. Isn't that what we all want? Have you thought about how to inject these elements into your own family, work group, church, or civic group?

I was overwhelmed, recently, when my daughter told me how much joy and love were coming out of her classroom where she was a teacher. She was living out these principles with the students, and the classroom had become a family. This sense of family really healed a number of these children. Her use of love, respect, resources, rules, routines, and responsibility changed them. This random group of little people was now a family full of love, cooperation, and support for one another.

One of my other daughters recently took a new leadership position in her company and included these ideas into her amazing leadership stuff. She saw huge gains in her new team, and a whole new atmosphere was created within her part of the company. I am so radically proud of both of these girls for harnessing their power and creating joy of "family" in a work setting. We all want and need to have some of our groups become more than just a random collection of individuals—*we need the joy of family.*

I realize this idea of family can mean many different things to different people. When I speak of the joy of family, what I mean is the harvest of good feelings and deeper connections with others. Each of us enjoys seeing others who want to be with us and who we want to be with. All of us feel good when we are respected for who we are and what we do. Everyone wants to be known by at least one group of people who will make sure we have all we need to thrive. In the game of life, there are rules to winning, and we love those who kindly and graciously help us understand what they are for each separate part of life. Life can seem really confusing and overwhelming at times; we are so grateful to those who help us simplify the difficult bits down to the essential steps or routines. No one likes correction or hearing where they are messing up, but they are essential for growth, and if done with kindness, a clear desire for the other's benefit, and wisdom, then it produces success and joy.

One of my greatest joys is starting small groups through the church. I love to witness how many of these groups make the leap to the joy of family when I introduce the Six R's. It is always delightful when people who did not know each other before find they care deeply about the people in the group, connecting with them and forming unexpected bonds of love and encouragement. A men's group I am a part of is just now making this leap. Together, we are seeing God do miracles in our lives as we cheer each other on and hold each other accountable.

My hope is for you to experience the *joy of family* in whatever group you're involved in—where all members feel a sense of unity, value, cooperation, purpose, love, and support. But for the purposes of this book, I will be showing you specifically how to add these ingredients into your family at home. You'll get an idea of how to do this from examples and stories coming from both me and my wife, Dana, my wonderful bride of thirty-one years. Together, we have raised three amazing young women, who are each living out these six ideas uniquely. You will undoubtedly work out these six elements differently than my wife and I did for our children, but you will need to add them into your family and groups if you want to create the sense of "family" you crave. I hope you find these useful for the core of what you do with your family and the groups in your life.

For Dana and I, our main goal was to enjoy our children and do all we could to encourage them. We knew our mission was to send them into adulthood equipped to live a great life and make a positive difference for God and others. We used the Six R's, which are not just theories; they are proven by the scriptures and tested in real families. Whenever I share our plan with people who have already created a joy-filled family, they all say, "Yes, that is what we did. We just didn't call it that."

Each chapter will cover one of these elements, and we will provide practical ideas and examples from our own parenting experience, as well as from others. But first, we need to lay some groundwork. Before we can even begin to open up any of these crucial elements, we need to introduce a deliberate, predetermined time to develop and work out these Six R's in your family. We call it a "Weekly Staff Meeting."

Your Weekly Staff Meeting—Don't Skip This!

It is a well-known fact that any good company holds weekly organizational meetings to communicate and coordinate important business, assign roles, budget the resources, and evaluate what is working or not. Really, the weekly staff meeting is a planning tool used to maintain order and structure so the business can be successful. Families are no different. In a sense, a family is a business entity, so they should also have pre-established goals, assigned tasks, budgets to live by, ways to deal with needs that come up, and a way to determine what is working and what is not. My belief is that every set of parents, even single parents, need some type of weekly planning meeting.

I was talking with a young man the other day who was having trouble in his family. The children were causing all kinds of problems for he and his wife. I suggested that one of the ways to help his children was by working out a plan before each new week. He took my suggestion and came back amazed at how much it had improved the family. He and his wife were working together, and the kids were behaving better (not perfect, but much better). *They had hope for the first time in a while.*

When Dana and I had our three girls in the home, we held a "staff meeting" to go over the Six R's nearly every week. We made it a high priority and rarely missed it. It made things so much easier. We monitored how well we were doing as parents in these six areas, and how each of our girls were doing in them. These six topics allowed us to systematically cover the issues that can often slip through the cracks of a busy family.

Holding the staff meeting regularly brought peace and order to our home and gave us a doable, well-thought-out plan to raise our children. We made a chart with the Six R's, added our names and each of our children's names across the top, then discussed how each one was doing in each area. Pretty simple. We weren't looking for perfection, but improvements in each of these areas for each person. Even ourselves.

For our family, here is what our chart looked like:

	Parent 1 GIL	Parent 2 DANA	Child 1 JENESSA	Child 2 ABBEY	Child 3 GRACE
Relationship					
Respect					
Resources					
Rules					
Routines					
Responsibility					

We made a rule to only work on one issue per week per person. So together, we would decide which area to work on with which child, and how we were going to bring what was needed in that area to an acceptable place. For example, if we thought Jenessa needed help with showing respect because we were noticing tones of disrespect for us or a teacher, we came up with a plan to instruct and practice respect. If Abbey seemed distant, then we would work on the relationship area. If Grace was having a hard time cleaning up her toys, then we knew there were rules to focus on for that week. The focus changed from week to week.

Using the Six R's, we would ask these types of questions:

Relationship
Is love flowing between us and all the children?

Respect
Is everyone valued and knowing how to value others?

Resources
Is everyone supplied with the resources they need to thrive?

Rules
Is everyone aware of and conforming to both the family's rules and God's laws?

Routines
Is everyone learning and following the appropriate routines for their age?

Responsibility
Is everyone taking responsibility for their own choices and actions?

This outline allows you and your spouse to customize parenting for your family. It was always amazing to me how I would come into the meeting thinking we should work on a certain area with the oldest child or this other area with the middle child, but then after talking to Dana about it, we agreed on a much different and better plan. She saw things and heard things I wasn't aware of and vice versa. The scriptures say that a father should not exasperate his children (Eph. 6:4), and this staff meeting was a major way God used to keep me from that problem.

As in any family, there are always problem areas, so you need a systematic way to address all the various issues in your family. You can't attack them all at once. The weekly staff meeting will help. Since the Six R's are the essential ingredients of a great family, they should be the key focus of your parenting efforts.

Ray Johnston, the dynamic senior pastor of Bayside Church, was training his staff about how to be an effective parent. He mentioned how he and his wife, Carol, would sit down at a coffee shop weekly and plan out how they were going to handle the week and month ahead. This was their version of the weekly staff meeting. It gave them the ability to anticipate what they needed to do so they could stay ahead of the kids, especially when they were small. The point is, you need to find what works for you.

Single parents aren't exempt from this staff meeting, either. You also need a "planning" meeting to figure out how you are going to handle issues in the next week. You could include other trusted people in your life to discuss how to solve different issues so you are not always relying on your own thinking. A single parent's staff meeting could be stretched over the days of the week as you meet with your child's teacher, coach, youth pastor, and potentially even their friends' parents. There is great value in getting different perspectives.

I have found it so helpful to take time every week to sit down and think through the issues you are facing in that stage of your parenting. Ask questions about what is working, what isn't working, and who should be brought into this issue. The great problem is that single parents often feel alone in their parenting. Don't let it be the case for you. Get the help you need.

There is one young lady, a single parent, who asks me whenever she sees me at church, "How would you handle this issue?" I'm happy to help her, because I know her job is extra tough! We have a lively discussion for a few minutes and she adds or dismisses my thoughts to her family plan.

Six Steps for Your Weekly Staff Meeting

To initiate a weekly staff meeting into your family plan, here are six steps you can take to get started:

Step 1—Where and When?

Decide when and where you and your spouse will meet regularly each week. If you are already doing marital staff meetings, which I have recommended in some of my other books, then this meeting would fit into that meeting. It could be Saturday afternoons, Sunday evenings, Wednesday nights—whatever works best for both of you, so long as it is consistent. It should be held in a place where you can talk openly and also pray together. Dana and I always met at 1:00 on Saturday. Now that the kids are grown and gone, we meet at 4:00 on Sundays. The planning doesn't stop just because the kids don't live in our home anymore. They still need our love and guidance, and we still work on our own things.

Step 2—Make Your Chart

Make a master copy of a chart like the one above that can then be printed out for each meeting. You'll want to customize it for your family. Use this chart each week as a guide for discussion.

Step 3—Review the Previous Week

Take some time to review the previous week—how it went, what worked, what didn't, and if the same area needs more work this week. Go through each of the Six R's for both parents and each child. Share any new information with your spouse so you are on the same page.

Step 4—Decide on This Week's R

Once you have shared about the success and frustrations of last week, you can decide together which of the Six R's you think should be the focus for each person. Pray ahead of time or at the beginning of the meeting asking God to guide you in this. If you and your spouse have different opinions, and you will, then celebrate the wisdom in both people and pick one of the Six R's to focus on. You can always pick the other one the next week. Remember, you only have 936 weeks to help develop your child. Before you know it, eighteen to twenty-one years will have flown by, but I can assure you that any weekly investment in the Six R's will be worth it.

Step 5—Develop a Plan for That Week

For the area you have selected, decide how you want to focus on that area for that child that week. Think of practical examples and creative ways to instruct and guide. Assign task of who will handle what. I will provide more ideas in the coming chapters.

Step 6—Post Your Plan

Post your plan in a prominent place: by the phone, refrigerator, on the bathroom mirror, in the car, and so forth. Put it wherever both of you will see it and be reminded to work on that area throughout the week. When both parents are on the same plan, it is amazing how much can be accomplished.

Remember, the goal is to develop and build a family full of love where you can enjoy your children and send them into adulthood equipped to live a great life and make a positive difference. The goal is not to create perfect children, but rather loving, wise individuals who understand their place in your family and the world. Holding a weekly planning meeting is crucial to this.

Of course, wise parenting takes work, but raising great kids and enjoying them along the way is so worth it. Jump in and become a wise parent. Learn each of the Six R's and how to implement them. I hope you are already thinking about which ones are weak in your family and other groups, as well as ways you could begin adding more of a particular family element. They need to be added regularly and consistently for a family of joy to develop. Commit and stick to the weekly staff meeting, and remember to invite the Lord into your plans—pray for God to firm up and establish your plans for a better, more enjoyable family.

> May the favor of the Lord our God rest on us; establish the work of our hands for us—yes, establish the work of our hand.
>
> —Psalm 90:17 niv

1.
relationship

LET ME TELL YOU THE STORIES OF THREE FAMILIES.

Jim and Linda's little daughter, Elizabeth, was a little over two. Linda was home to watch when Elizabeth heard a plane fly over the house and she rushed to the window to wave at the plane. "Bye, daddy!" she said. Linda's heart broke, realizing that Elizabeth completely associated airplanes with her father because he was always getting on one. Jim and Linda knew they needed to make some changes if they were going to create a family of joy. Jim recognized that if he provided every monetary benefit but did not provide himself to his family, then his family wouldn't work. It took a while, but they changed numerous things in each of their work schedules and overall busy-ness to prioritize Jim's presence with Linda and Elizabeth. They are on their way to experiencing the joy of family.

John and Laura had two daughters who they loved very much. John worked a lot; Laura was busy with community activities, and the girls had school. It was the typical suburban-American family. They did not suspect anything was wrong with their family until their oldest was fifteen. She met a young man at school, and at first it looked like a normal, teenage romance. But in less than a month, she was pregnant, had dropped out of school, and was living at her boyfriend's parents' house. Her parents were devastated; this relationship was different than the ones they had in high school, and now the lack of loving bonds in their family were exposed. There had not been enough relationship, respect, and resources within the family to cause their daughter to want to stay, so she left for the other family.

John and Laura did everything they could think of to reconnect with their daughter, but nothing worked. Three years later, when their younger daughter turned fifteen, I noticed the same patterns beginning, and I asked to see John. I told him that I believed he had less than two weeks to intensify his love and respect for his daughter and remove her from the romantic and school situation she was in or else her love and allegiance could also be swept away. Because of what had happened before, he immediately pulled his daughter from her school and put her in a different one where he and his wife would be much more involved. It worked, and the open love and joy in their family blossomed. In the meantime, John began a different approach for loving his oldest daughter. Over the course of five years, they were able to restore their relationship, allowing the family to assist this new mom and enjoy their granddaughter.

David came to see me about a crisis that was happening with his son, Joel. When Joel was fourteen, he began to really struggle in school. And, come to find out, he was being valued, loved, and groomed by an older teen to embrace a new sexual identity. Joel was pushing away from the values the family had embraced and was wrestling with his identity as a young man. As David and I talked, I suggested that in many of these types of cases, it was often the relationship with the father that made a huge difference. I suggested that he intensify his relationship with his son: take him to the movies, go on boat trips, go to Disneyland, volunteer to coach his baseball team, and any other thing that sounded fun. David did all that and more. He told me six months later that all the bizarre, destructive behavior had disappeared as the relationship with Dad had increased. It was a miracle. Children need a real relationship with their parents, not just food and shelter.

I don't mean to suggest that any of the above situations were easily remedied, but the addition of significant levels of relationship (love) can make an almost miraculous difference in a child's life.

THE POWER OF RELATIONSHIP

Children need a relationship with their parents that is deep and obvious to everyone involved. It is hard to overstate how important the power of relationship is in your children's life. It is everything to them. *You* are everything to them. God has placed each child in a family so he or she will be cared for, loved, and trained. This child needs your love. This child needs your instruction about the world and how to succeed at life. Children can overcome lots of things (poverty, injustice, inadequate schooling) if they have love from their parents. You will not be perfect, but if you give the love, then you put in the heart of your child an unstoppable force.

This chapter deals with how to insert ways to build relationship with your children—to increase the love quotient so they will feel your love, support, and value of them. God has entrusted you and your spouse with these children. Your role as a parent is to love them as they grow older and introduce others into their life who will also love them. You don't need me to tell you to hug your kids, listen to them, enjoy them, be with them, teach them, or protect them. You already know to do these things. They are precious and you know it. Your love is enough for them if you give it to them in a way that they can receive it. Even if you are a single mom or a single dad and you feel overwhelmed, it is your love that will reach into the heart of each child and help them so much.

Family is about love.

If there is enough love, family works. Children desperately need to know, feel, and see demonstrations of love so they are sure their parents love them. God tells us how to do this. Malachi 4:6 tells us it is important for the hearts of the parents to be focused on the children. God will work on the father to turn his heart toward his children, because he knows it is crucial for fathers to stay engaged in their lives. Titus 2:3, 4 instructs moms to learn how to love their children. This is not the sacrificial love which moms are so good at… it is the friendship love that needs to be developed, the kind that really *likes* the children. First Corinthians 15:33 tells us that bad company will corrupt good morals, so one of the things parents must make sure of is that the types of people your children are around will reinforce the positive life you hope for your children. The Bible is full of parenting advice if we are tuned in.

FATHERS, YOU MATTER!

If I may, I would like to take the opportunity to talk directly to the dads out there. Statistics are pouring in on the issue of how important fathers are in the development of boys and girls. It is actually debated these days if fathers are important beyond their paycheck. That's ludicrous! The answer is *yes!* It is absolutely crucial for fathers to stay engaged and active in their children's lives. The greatest single cause of whether children will take the right moral road is the connection they have with their father. An absentee father predicts teen pregnancy and gun violence in 86+ percent of the cases… (emotions, distance, divorce). At the time of this writing, these are the statistics I received from Focus on the Family.[1]

- 63% of youth suicides are from fatherless homes;
- 90% of all homeless children and runaways are from fatherless homes;

- 80% of rapists motivated by displaced anger come from fatherless homes;
- 71% of all high school dropouts come from fatherless homes;
- 75% of all adolescent patients in chemical abuse centers come from fatherless homes;
- 85% of all youths sitting in prisons grew up in a fatherless home.

Dads, you matter. These statistics show it! Stay engaged and keep parenting even though it is difficult. I know it is. Keep going. Families matter, and families need a mom and a dad who both care for and love the children.

Let me add one more thing that is forgotten in our day but crucial in the life of your children: *the Father's Blessing.* A man's children desperately need him to be proud of them. And to hear him say it. I try to regularly let my children know by texts and phone calls what I am proud of them for and how excited I am about the life they are building. You can do this too. If you'd like more about this, I can recommend two great books to read: *Intentional Manhood* by Coach Mike Stanley and *Raising a Modern Day Knight* by Robert Lewis. Check them out and keep learning.

3 Ways to Develop Relationship in Your Family

When we want to develop a relationship with another person, we do it through one or more channels:

1. Work with them.
2. Talk with them.
3. Play with them.

These are basically the only three ways I know of to develop a relationship. In fact, I would go so far to say this is how you found the person you married. Different people will enjoy or utilize different ones of these but each is necessary to build relationships. With parenting, doing one of these three things with your child will help you build strong bonds with them.

It's the second word that is crucial. The word *"with."* We live in a day and age when everybody is trying to multi-task, so we try and get the children to clean their rooms while we work on something different in the garage. That does not build relationships. It gets things done, but what your kids need is to be with you seeing you work, watching them work, talking with them, listening to them talk, playing with you and having you watch them play. Relationships may be inefficient entities, but they do something in our soul that is vital. I say they are inefficient because it takes two or more people doing something that one person could really do by themselves. But the point is relational. We are social creatures; we want to be around people whom we love and who love us; that's how we build lives of joy. Strong relationships are essential to us thriving and being happy.

My father built a relationship with me by making me do chores with him. We would build fences, fix cars, make furniture, and other such things. He also had me go fishing with him which he found very exciting. My wife's family always took her out for breakfast on Saturday morning to talk. They were all about talking, and it built a great relationship between them. I found that my children loved to go on dates with me and play sports. We developed a bond through playing together. Ask yourself: "How am I building a relationship with each of my children? Am I working with them, talking with them, playing with them?"

Spend time finding the "with" activity that works for you. My father was not huge with the "talk with" piece, so he spent time working with me and playing with me. This was great, and he remains one of my best friends as an adult. I know of one father who developed and maintained his relationship with his boys through his wallet. He bought dirt bikes when the boys were small and they would go to the desert and ride. It was glorious for them. When the boys got tired of dirt bikes, he sold them and bought jet skis and took the boys to the lake. I remember when the oldest boy was about eighteen, he asked his father if he could take the jet skis to the lake with some of his friends. His father very wisely said, "Those jet skis are my jet skis, so if you are inviting me to bring my jet skis to the lake with a group of your friends, let's go. But if you want to take my jet skis to the lake without me, that won't work." His son quickly corrected, saying, "Dad, of course we wanted you to come and enjoy time at the lake with me and my friends." This dad knew what he was doing.

Your kids need at least an hour of your presence each day. Here are some practical ideas that worked for us in each of the three areas:

Work with...

Homework: Help them with their homework for a few minutes so that you know what they are working on. Talk about whether it is hard or easy and how they like that subject. Don't do their homework for them but relate to them during some portion of their homework time. Maybe even work on something of your own, like read a book, pay some bills, or do a Bible study. The key is being near them and available while they do their work.

Help them clean or organize their room: Each of my children were less motivated to do chores when they were expected to do them by themselves. Join them in cleaning their rooms. Make it fun and use incentives to motivate them. Use the time to talk, remember, and teach about the importance of an organized space and cleaning out.

Yardwork or repairs: Kids need to know how to do practical things, like rake the leaves, mow the grass, or fix things around the house. Invite them to join you and let them participate as their age allows. Teach them how to use a hammer, a screwdriver, using the time to explain how things work. Give them tasks to do and praise them even if they don't do things perfectly.

Serve together: Doing something kind for others is a great bonding tool. It doesn't have to be big things either, like serving the homeless or going on a mission. It can be preparing and delivering a meal for someone in need, baking cookies for a neighbor, or taking old magazines to a nursing home. Be creative and allow you children to come up with ideas of their own.

Talk with...

Dinner time (talking around the table): We made a big deal out of having a family dinner each evening, and a part of that process was talking and catching up with each other. It is fascinating to me hearing about what the kids and my wife experienced that day. And I love hearing the answers to questions like, "What was the most memorable (or fun, exciting, boring, and so on) thing about today for you?"

Late-night talks: Most children will talk to their parents late at night (especially if it allows them to stay up later). I arranged my schedule to stay up late and talk with my children individually each week or so. They were willing to tell me how their life was really going and what their problems were during these late-night sessions. I got a real window into their soul and their life because of listening to them after we put them to bed. Try not to rush this process.

Family devotions: We used dinner time to have family devotion about a key Bible passage. I made up placemats that had all the key passages on them: the Ten Commandments, the Lord's Prayer, the Beatitudes, the Fruit of the Spirit, the Great Commandments. (See appendix 2.) Then I would ask a question like, "Did you see anyone violate one of the Ten Commandments today?" "Did you use any of the fruit of the Spirit today?" I would also have us read or recite together one of the passages. Every night, I went over the Ten Commandments because moral understanding is absolutely crucial. I used articles from the paper or something I was reading and asked them which commandment it related to. The whole thing lasted about five to ten minutes each night, but it was valuable in talking through issues and helping them tie together real-life situations to ancient commandments. It also built our relationship with our kids.

Play with…

Yogurt runs: We went out to have frozen yogurt during the summer as a way to be together. You might have some kind of dessert routine that works for your family. It is all a way to be together and discuss something different and enjoy one another at a low cost.

Sports and teams: Our culture is sports crazy as though being on a sports team will solve everything. It really can be a great way of spending time with your kids that is fun and enjoyable for everybody. But if it stops being a time with your children or stops being enjoyable for the children or parents, then find something else to do. Remember that the point of sports is to help families not tear them apart. Your children need their family more than they need to know how to kick a soccer ball or field a grounder.

I remember one couple who felt that their two children were not focusing and being calm, so they enrolled the whole family into archery lessons. The family did archery for years, and it taught the kids how to focus and still their mind. Their grades improved, and their ability to handle stress increased. We enrolled our children in swimming because it kept us all around the same pool interacting with our kids.

Date nights: Take each child on a date each week for an hour. Listen to what they want to talk about. Go down to the store and let them buy something. Go to the park and just sit on the bench or throw a ball around, and let them have special time with you.

These are just a few ideas, and I'm sure you have some of your own. Take a minute and jot down a few that come to the top of your head. Commit to doing these things with your kids, and get ready for the relationships to grow.

Relationships that Determine Your Kids' Future Direction—Good or Bad

Many parents do not understand that their children tend to identify with groups of people and individuals, and when they do, they will automatically become like those groups and individuals. That's why you want to make sure that the people they identify with are good people who will pull them toward the good side of life. There are about twelve to fourteen relationships your children have or will have as they develop. Some are with real people, but many are formed with sources of input or fictional characters in books or games. Parents need to know what relationships their child has and how to harness them for the good of their children.

One of the consistent things I say to parents I am coaching is, "If your children are going sideways in some way, then there is a toxic relationship dripping poison into your child's life. Find the relationship, find the toxic substance, and eliminate it. I guarantee you will get your child back." I have seen this happen over and over again. It may be a friend. It may be their new music. It may be a teacher or older friend. It may be a boyfriend or girlfriend. It may be a movie or video game or social media. Yes, I understand that some children handle these issues well, but your child is being influenced in some negative way if they are changing in a damaging way. Find the relationship and change it to eliminate the toxic portion, or eliminate the relationship altogether.

Let's get into the most basic relationships kids have these days. It should start with you, the parents.

Father and Mother

As I noted earlier, there have been numerous studies conducted that continually prove parents as the most powerful influence in their child's life. Parents often don't feel powerful, and they squander the power they do have to influence them positively. Your children need you to be a source for goodness in their life. They need you to be cheering for them, not always telling them what they did wrong or that they could do better. Yes, you will have to tell them they were wrong sometimes, and of course you cannot support criminal behavior, but let them know you are for them, even if they did a bad thing.

The relationship between you and your kids will change as they go through puberty and on towards adulthood, but you still have a responsibility to foster a relationship with your children. Your children will eventually need to express independence from you, but you get to pick the time and place for that to happen. Being a parent means you are the leader, the authority, and the adult in the room. There will be times when you don't know what to do and will need input from others and even from your children, but that does not mean you can or should abandon the parent role. Yes, you will be wrong at times and you can apologize, but do not abdicate being the parent your children need. Yes, your children will know more about technology and what is cool in the present culture, but you are still the parent. And do not give up the parenting role and just become their friend (that comes after twenty-one).

Also, it is imperative that you be the parent who protects your children from any form of abuse (physical, mental, emotional, sexual). Do not allow a spouse, a coach, or anybody else abuse or bully your children. There are no excuses for allowing another adult or child to do this. I have watched too many spouses try and explain to me why they had to allow abuse to continue. I know it is tough to tell someone who can put a stop to it. I know that it will damage and potentially destroy your family, but you must let people know who can help. Your children need your protection and your advocacy. Parents who have stepped in and alerted the right authorities have come out on the other side so much better. Do not allow abuse under any circumstances.

Mentors and Role Models

Work diligently to connect your child with positive mentors and role models. Every child should have someone other than you to help guide them when they can't hear the wisdom of their parents, or who can provide wisdom the parents don't have. Your children will need people beyond you if they are going to be completely ready for the adult world. They will need other adults who know more than you and say the same things you do in a different way. Your children will need to see that you are not the only person who thinks and acts the way you do.

Through the late elementary years and teen years, wise parents look for people who will reinforce the behavior and character they want to instill in their children. You should look for coaches, teachers, music instructors, tutors, youth pastors, dance instructors, guidance counselors, or even a family member, such as a grandparent, uncle or aunt, even a neighbor, who will guide your children in a hundred details of their life. I can remember hiring great young ladies to lead a Bible study or teach my girls guitar because I wanted my girls to see how a great young lady behaved as they got older. I knew that my girls may not be willing to listen to my wife and I on particular topics, but they might listen to these ladies. These young ladies made an impact on our girls, and we are grateful.

Friends

Your children will have all kinds of friends as they grow up. You want to make sure that ideas and choices their friends have are in line with the things you support. If you allow your child to spend a lot of time with a young man or a young woman who does things you don't allow, the child will be tempted to make the same bad choices. I spent a lot of time praying, picking out schooling, and arranging sports so that the kind of friends we wanted our children to hang out with would be available to them. What was interesting is that many of my children did not make friends at church, but they did make friends at school or at sports practices. It doesn't matter who it is so long as they are the type of friends who will help you instill the right kind of boundaries in your child.

Eliminate unhealthy relationships (subtly if possible). If your child becomes involved with an unhealthy friend, take subtle but effective steps to remove that friend from their life. My wife and I were always on the lookout for friends who were into drugs, parties, rebellion, and criminality, and we worked hard to get that friend away from our kid. We did things like not take our child to a gathering if that person would be there; we prayed earnestly against that person for God to remove them out of our kid's life; we booked a family outing on the evening when that group was going to meet for a party, and so forth. It often only takes a few weeks or a month to cement an unhealthy relationship, so be vigilant.

I can remember one time at the dinner table when one of my daughters told the family that many of her friends were moving away or not coming back to the school the next year. I raised my hand and said, "That would be my fault." My daughter asked, "What do you mean?" I said, "I thought that those friends were bad influences on your life so I prayed them out of your life." I explained how I had prayed and how God was simply answering my prayers. Everyone realized that dad is protecting and praying, and God is listening.

Romance

Your children might have romances during their teen years. Be positive about their new feelings. If you are always against these feelings and experiences, you build walls between you and your children exactly where you need bridges and dialogue. Let them know that they will have these feelings and what to do with them responsibly. Tell them that these feelings will come and go sometimes very quickly. Teach them that they cannot put their feelings in the driver's seat. They need to keep their head when making decisions. They cannot hand over the controls of their life to their heart as much of our culture is telling kids. Don't follow your heart; follow your head, and more importantly, the Lord Jesus.

Don't let some romance steal your child away. If a young man or a young woman is really wrong for your child, have a talk with your child before it goes on too long. Also be willing to have a conversation with the other young person. Let them know that they are not in charge; you are still protecting and watching. I can remember having a conversation with one of my daughter's boyfriends where I let him know what he could and could not do. I also let him know that when it was over, he needed to man up and let her know personally. I was very grateful he had followed through on my advice and called her when he no longer had any feelings for her. I was holding my daughter as she was hearing him break up with her on the phone.

Being there with your children is better than preventing every little scrape or difficulty. They need to see you care in the midst of real life. You can be the most supportive, confidential, wise, comforting adult relationship your children have. They need to have you in their corner. They expect you to defend and protect them and to want their best.

God

Showing your child how to have a real relationship with God is one of the most important responsibilities a parent has. They need to know how to read the Bible and hear the Lord speak through it. They need to learn to pray and watch God answer, how to confess their sins and sense God's forgiveness. Knowing how to serve the Lord and feel the pleasure of God when they do is tremendously valuable, as well as knowing how to worship and adore God and sense His presence. Teach your children how to practice the spiritual disciplines so that their faith can be their own instead of an extension of your faith. I wrote *Spiritual Disciplines of a C.H.R.I.S.T.I.A.N.* to help young Christians know and enjoy a real relationship with God and grow in love with Him.

Each of my children were led to a saving knowledge of the Lord Jesus Christ at a Red Robin restaurant at around four years of age. All children, as they grow, go through mental developmental stages. Their brains process things differently at ages two to five, then it changes and they can process more until they are nine to twelve. They go to another stage from thirteen to fifteen where abstract thinking works, then they go through another mental stage at sixteen to nineteen. I believe that your children need to receive Jesus at each stage of their development. They are like a new person at each stage, and they need to be able to understand and embrace Jesus at each new mental age. That is why many children will report they rededicated their life to Christ at seventeen or so, and it felt like they were not even a Christian before in light of what it now means.

As a parent, you need to make sure your children ask their questions and have experiences and prayers that are appropriate to that mental developmental stage. I have watched too many college-age people give up on their faith because they are trying to believe in the Jesus they heard about when they were seven. Their seven-year-old concept of Jesus will not be sufficient for the world and questions of a twenty-year-old.

Siblings

Siblings impact each other immensely. A great and understanding brother or sister is an incredible blessing. An evil brother or sister paves a road for destruction for all the other brothers and sisters. Work hard with the sibling dynamic and understand it. Younger children may be being bullied in your own family, so you need to find a way for them to tell you what is really going on with and to them. You need to know if something destructive is happening. Your children will not necessarily be best friends, but they should not be sworn enemies.

Help your children have the tools to talk to one another and show them how to disagree and still relate deeply. Youngest children often have very little opportunity or means to speak to the powers in their life. The dynamics of older siblings hearing rebukes from the younger ones is very helpful. Show your kids how to disagree without having to win or damage the relationship. They need to know how to apologize and how to repair and restart the relationship. We found that we had to show our children how mom and dad disagreed and how we worked through the issue so that they could see how we did it. Help them work through disagreements with their brothers and sisters.

Also, be very careful when you change the dynamic of your family. While adopting a child can be very rewarding and even save a child's life, it affects the biological children too in profound ways. Seek to understand those issues. Also, be very careful about who you bring into your home. A child that is trained in evil will train your children in evil. Many times, the parents are immune from the evil but the children are not.

Music

Your children will also have a relationship with the music you allow them to play. A wise parent will develop a policy on music that makes sense for both spouses. If your current music policy, or lack of one, seems to encourage rebellion, then change it or add one. I find that a significant part of the rebellion of adolescence is strengthened by the music a young person is playing. If the rebellious music is pulled, then the child tends to drop much of the rebellious defiance in a week or two.

I remember one young lady who was incredibly defiant to her parents, and they became increasingly troubled. Because the defiance moved toward extremely dangerous behavior, I suggested they pull their daughter out of school, put her on independent study for the rest of the semester, and not allow her to listen to the music she had been listening to. In three to four weeks, the transformation was astounding. When the parents told me, I could see they had their daughter back. You don't have to let your children pick what they want to listen to, and you should certainly know who they are listening to. Also, you should know what those musicians stand for and what they are singing about. Read the lyrics and look up their story on the internet.

We were fairly strict in this area. I'm not advocating our family's music policy unless this makes sense to you and your spouse. We had two standards as the girls were growing up. Up until they were sixteen, they could listen to Christian music. If it wasn't Christian music, then they couldn't listen to it. When they turned sixteen, they could expand their musical tastes to a broader scope than just the Christian genre, but they had to determine if the person was singing about truth and righteousness. The person did not have to be Christian, but they did need truth and righteousness themes and values in their lyrics. I would not suggest that you necessarily adopt the standard that we did for our children, and definitely not if they have never been exposed to this type of standard before. But I do think that parents should be aware of what their children are listening to and restrict the music if it advocates behaviors that are destructive to them.

Movies

One of the things that movies are designed to do is to get the audience to identify with the characters in the movies. Your children will have favorite movies because they see themselves in one of the characters. You really want to understand which movies they are enjoying and which characters they are they connecting with. I remember I was helping one mom and dad with their teenage children, and I was talking about movies with the youngest daughter. She said she really liked a particular movie. "Oh great!" I asked, "What did you like about the movie?" She then told me all about a particularly evil character in the movie who practiced occult ceremonies, killed people, and was really twisted by evil. That led to quite a discussion about Satanic power and the nature of evil to distort and destroy. It was very helpful for the young lady to talk about these things rather than let her embrace the character as an icon in her mind. I have found that most children want to discuss their favorite movies with their parents if their parents will actually discuss the movie with them. Don't just blast their favorite character but discuss, suggest real-world consequences, and be willing to look further at the implications of a movie or character.

Not everyone will adopt the standards that our family used on films. Some are stricter than my wife and I, and some are looser than we were. Probably the most important thing I would say we did was we watched the movies with our kids so that we could discuss them rather than let the images just go into their minds. We used our discernment with the ratings systems to help our girls know which movies they could watch and which ones they could not. We did not let them watch PG-13 movies until they were thirteen and then only select ones. We don't watch R-rated movies (with the exception of *The Passion of the Christ*), so we did not let our children watch them either. I watched many movies with my girls as they were turning twelve and then thirteen so that we could discuss the content and messages of movies with them. This was a really great time spent with each of the girls as they grew older. I would take them through a whole host of movies that they would not have known to watch and it helped us discuss all kinds of subjects.

Television

There are many different approaches to television viewing, but I want you to be aware that your children will develop relationships with the characters and shows they view on television. Make sure they are watching programs that move them toward responsibility and wise behavior. There are television shows and channels that are trying to move children to accept unrighteous and immoral actions as normal and accepted. Be aware of this fact and decide how you will handle this.

I have found that many parents who restrict their children from all TV create a sensational appetite for any kind of television in their children. There is almost an insatiable hunger for TV that is also unhealthy. Television viewing is one of those areas where children must be taught and trained over the years to view it responsibly. How much can be viewed and still get all the chores and homework done? What kinds of shows cause nightmares and which ones don't? How long does it take to do bedtime rituals well and really be ready for sleep? What is better than television (time with friends, hobbies, sports, game with parents, and so forth)?

Magazines

This may not be true as much as it was in the past but some magazines are aimed at developing a relationship with your children to influence the way they think, and more importantly, what they purchase. We did not allow our children to read or subscribe to secular teenage magazines because I could not guarantee what was in them. A good magazine with interesting articles can always be a treat and something for special occasions. I have seen teenagers who will take the word of an advice columnist in a magazine over their parents just because it is in a magazine. It should also be noted that if you as parents have a lot of magazines that would be inappropriate reading material for your children, you should be careful where the magazines are left. I am not a fan of parents having material that would be corrupting to the children in the home. I have heard too many stories of young boys who got a hold of their father's pornography collection or young girls who read articles that were immoral. These are incredibly corrupting to young teenage minds.

Computer/Internet

One of the strongest relationships that parents and children must have an understanding about is using the computer and the internet. The computer can be a wonderful tool for the advancement of your children's learning. But it can also be a source of bullying, corruption, immorality, lies, and fear. There are some ground rules to put in place when it comes to computers and the internet. The computer should be accessed in a public part of the house not in a child's room. Everything on the computer should be viewable by the parents, everything. You can install a software program that monitors every website and sends a report to the parents. Children are way too trusting and can be very naïve for online predators of all kinds. There should just not be any question about the fact that parents can see and know all the information on the computer and browsing history. This will not be a problem unless a child has been given too much freedom early and then in the teen years transparency is demanded.

There are other parental controls on the computer and the internet to research and implement. The field changes so fast that any specific programs I would suggest here would be obsolete by the time this book is printed. Talk to tech-savvy people you know about the best way to have your children benefit from the computer without the dangers that come with it. You would not let a robber or predator into your home to be with your child in their bedroom, so you should not let them come through the computer either. Monitor everything.

Social Media

There are tremendous pressures on children from social media and mobile platforms. As parents, you get to decide how fully your children should have access to the various social media platforms. The key here is full transparency. Whatever level you allow your children to have access to social media platforms, it should come with full openness to the parents or else it is not allowed. The parents may not post on it, but they are silent witness to everything. Be mindful that sometimes kids have multiple accounts under different nicknames—one that is more cleaned up so parents and other adults can see it, and one that is more hidden and for kids their own age. In many cases, your child may be sensitive to the peer pressures of social media and it will be necessary to get them off of this intense peer-pressure channel. Do not hesitate to do what is best for your child. Every child wants to fit in, and their peer group tells them how to do that...but that is not often the best way to fit in. Make sure that you as their parents are loving and valuing them so that they get the most affirmation from you.

We restricted our children from the social media platforms of their day. They were not allowed by the rules of the social media providers to be on the platform before fourteen years of age. So we started there. Then we did all we could to monitor all the traffic on it. We also restricted the amount of time the kids could be on it. Thankfully my girls realized how intense the peer pressure was from their friends and chose to fast from social media periodically. They just accepted that they would not know the latest news immediately. We talked about this all the time. There are better programs out there now that will allow a parent to know what is happening online on their child's phone or computer... take advantage of these. Don't hide the fact that you are using it... make it known and obvious. This is the right of the parent to love their children in these ways. If you are paying for the phone or computer or internet, then you should know what is being consumed.

Video Games

Another area that can develop into a relationship and even an addiction is video games. A wise parent knows what video games their child is playing or even plays the games with them. You are the one who approves or disapproves of the games. Again, this requires transparency about how much time the game is played and that the games are played after the homework and chores are done. There should be a set number of hours games can be played. Remember you are trying to get your children to make great choices in this area and not just have you as their warden. There are programs that will monitor times and give you a rating or description of the various games.

One of the dangers of video games is that they are everywhere and if your house monitors the amount of time on the game but their friend's house doesn't, then they will spend all their time over at their friend's house. This means that the time at the friend's house must be monitored in the same way as the video game. If you allow two hours on the game, then you allow two hours at the friend's house. Just assume that the game is being played over there. If not, then so much the better. Your assignment as parents is to make sure that your child has a rich and fully developed mental, emotional, spiritual, physical, and relational life. Too much time focused on only one activity or one friend stifles that. Parent them lovingly and positively and be their biggest advocate.

In our home we just never got around to buying a game console until the girls were grown up. It was a way to not have the hassle of saying it was time to get off the game. Video games are very common but they are not a right of teens. We played plenty of other kinds of games, and they had sports and homework to keep them occupied.

Books

Another area that can be either a great source for good or a source for corruption is the whole area of books. Help your children find good books to read. You should encourage your children to read. But it must be more than just reading. I did not want my children reading books that glorified evil or taught the specifics of evil. I wanted them to read books about people of faith, about people who pushed back against evil. I wanted my children to develop identifications with real heroes who made a difference. I also did not want my girls to read a lot of books that glorified romance or following their heart. One of the worst possible sayings for a teenager to embrace is "Follow your heart." I have repeated over and over in every way I can how destructive following your emotions can be. "Follow your head." Stay objective, feel your feelings, but don't let them lead.

Conclusion

The area of relationship is so crucial. They really do control the future of your children's life. We will become like the people who love us and who we love. It is important as parents that your children are loved and feel your love for them. Yes, you have to correct them, but it should be clear that your love is overwhelming and always wants their best interest. They have to know in their bones that you really like them and value them as individuals. Take the time to work with them, talk with them, and play with them. Yes, it is not the most fun thing you can think to do at the time in a number of cases, but it is an investment in their future and your future. Nothing you can do is more important than developing a relationship with them of love.

Your love for them must always be clearly more than your instruction, training, and correction, or you run the risk that they will rebel. How can they rebel, though, from older people who love them and clearly like being with them and always have their best interest at heart? They won't rebel from love. Everybody needs it. Talk with them about the junior high romances that are everything to them. Don't tell them that these will pass. Talk with them as individuals who are in their moment of anguish or exhilaration. Let them work with you on real projects that really matter. Great things will come up and you will communicate how important they are to you.

My father use to let me do real work on the car, on the furniture, and in the yard, and he lived with my mess ups and limited skills. It always spoke to me that he would let me really help when I was little. Play with your children and enjoy every phase of their growing up. Throw yourself into the moment they are in and don't wish that they were older and could enjoy your thing. Get into their thing and explore their feelings, thoughts, and actions. It will be a wonderful way to get to know them and love them.

There will be a time in your life when you will desperately want a relationship with your children, and they will give you a relationship usually at the level that you gave to them when they were small. So many times we are chasing fame from the world but God would have us chase fame with our children. Become famous to them and see life work.

QUESTIONS TO ASK AT THE WEEKLY STAFF MEETING:

- How is our relationship looking?
- How is our relationship with each child?
- What could improve our relationship with each child? Work with? Talk with? Play with?
- What new relationship do we need to add to our kids?
- What relationship do we need to monitor?
- What relationship do we need to eliminate?
- Are they too connected to TV, movies, books, music, magazines, social media, video games? Which ones?
- What is our Music/TV/Media Policy? How are we enforcing it?
- What is our Computer/Internet/Social Media/Gaming Policy? How are we enforcing it?

2. respect

CHILDREN NEED TO KNOW THEY are WONDERFUL, SPECIAL, SIGNIFICANT, AND EXTREMELY VALUABLE TO YOU. While most parents *feel* these things about their kids, they don't necessarily do a great job of conveying it. Kids tend to experience more negative direction and words than positive reinforcement and praise.

I remember one couple who was having a real struggle with their thirteen-year-old daughter. This girl was going through the normal adolescent-independence phase, but then something happened that moved her to talk about running away. I had the opportunity to speak with the young girl, and after lots of questions and honesty, she told me that recently, when her mother was angry with her, her mother yelled, "I love you, but I don't like you." This statement destroyed the girl, because in a thirteen-year-old's world, to "like" someone is more powerful than to love them. Her mother's declaration cut at the heart of one of the things she needed most: *value*.

As parents, we are probably guilty of saying something we didn't mean or using words that came across harsher than we intended. Let's face it—kids can drive us crazy! But one of the things children desperately need is the sense that they are valuable. How valuable?

Valuable enough their parents want to spend time with them.

Valuable enough to be complimented and praised.

Valuable enough to be treated nicely and with kindness.

Children are watching for all of these clues. The way their parents treat them says something about their worth, significance, and value. They watch the parents show deference and value and respect to other people, things, and events, and they desperately want to be treated that way as well.

Think of it this way: all of us are like flowers turning toward the sun. We all naturally move in the direction of those who respect, praise, and encourage us. Your children are no different. They will discount people who constantly notice their flaws and failings, and call as friends those who trumpet their strengths and victories. If the people who do so are immoral people, then your child will have immoral friends.

This is a truth to live by:

> *All of us are drawn toward people who notice our strengths, celebrate our victories, and minimize our mistakes and weaknesses.*

This is what valuing someone looks like.

Value and respect are synonymous; they go hand in hand. This chapter highlights the desperate need in all families for both of these qualities. Respect equals value, and we reveal how much we value someone by the way we treat or respect them. We show respect to the people we greatly value by the way we honor them, listen to them, take their ideas and worries seriously, and consider their point of view when making decisions. People we don't value or respect are given few or none of these things.

For kids, the primary sources for respect (especially in the early years) should be their family members. Scripture says, "Honor your father and mother" (Eph. 6:2). But it also says, "Train up a child in the way he should go, even when he is old he will not depart from it" (Prov. 22:6). The first Scripture tells kids they need to honor (respect, add value to) their parents, but they don't inherently know how to do this. We must teach them how to respect us, as well as their friends and siblings. We do this not only by teaching them what respect is and what it looks like, but by the way we treat them and by our example in the way we treat others. A healthy home is one where respect is practiced, and each person is regarded with importance and value. It starts with you, mom and dad.

I want you to know how important it is for your children to receive the most praise, encouragement, and value from you, the parents. If you are overly negative, the danger is that they will move away from you and your guiding influence. It is very easy in the parenting process to keep pointing out their failings and weaknesses and difficulties. But while it is important to help children grow to maturity, correct their mistakes, and help them become well-rounded, it is more important to celebrate their unique contributions, talents, and strengths.

Having watched numerous families get this area wrong and other wonderful families get this really right, Dana and I worked hard to compliment our children every day. We would stop them when they were doing something right and tell them what we saw, that we were proud of them for it; we would show them we were excited to see them when they came home each day; we found time to listen to them when they wanted to talk. All of this was a concerted effort to demonstrate value and respect. We both agreed that we wanted our children to feel more valued by us than any friend ever would, and it worked to help us have a very joyful and encouraging family.

Parents largely determine how close their children are to them by the level of appreciation, praise, and encouragement they give their children. All of us need this, and children need it more. Draw your children towards you through praise and encouragement, so that they will listen to your advice and direction. Make sure they receive more respect, praise, and appreciation from you than from anyone else.

Let me give you fifteen practical ways you can demonstrate respect to your children. Some of these you may already be doing; if so, keep up the great work! There may be some you've never thought of trying. See if some of these new ideas can be implemented in your home.

15 Ways to Demonstrate Respect

1. **Pay a compliment to each child every day.** Each one of your children need to hear a personal, positive word spoken towards them on a daily basis. Catch them doing something good and point it out to them. Stop them and tell them you love them. I realize it is easier to notice what they didn't do or what they did wrong, but in the long run, constant talk about the negative will not build an enjoyable family. Make sure your children know you are more likely to stop them and tell them something good about their life than to correct them. I heard that the ratio of positive to negative comments should be ten to one; that is ten positive comments to one negative or critical comment. This could be quite a challenge, but it is one we need to practice. I enjoyed stopping my girls to say, "Did you see what you just did there? That was terrific. Keep doing that!" Who wouldn't want to be around someone who always points out the good things they do? I know I would.

2. **Point out their strengths.** I can remember one of my girls was having a tough day because of something happening at school. I told her that she was terrific. She looked at me and said, "How am I terrific?" She needed specif-

ics and I needed to go from the general things I found terrific about her to details that made her special. It really put me on the spot, but we sat down and I was able to point out over ten specifics that everyone recognized about her. She glowed after hearing the list. It can be helpful to keep a written or mental list of the positive abilities, skills, and temperament traits that each child shows. It can even be good to have it on the refrigerator so the kids can see you are noticing what they are good at.

If you are having trouble noticing their strengths because of the messy room and the way they do their chores, take a step back and look at where they excel. Talk to their teachers, ask their friends what they like about them, talk to coaches and specialty instructors and tutors and let them tell you about your child. Your child is a gift from God to you in a number of ways, and you need to keep that perspective even when they are going through a disruptive period. Remember, children tend to have good periods and then disruptive periods, then a good period, and so on, all through their eighteen years with you. It's normal.

3. **Use your words to build them up.** Words are valuable. The scriptures say, "Let no unwholesome word proceed from your mouth, but only such a word as is good for edification" (Eph. 4:29). In fact, death and life are in the power of the tongue (Prov. 18:21)! Your children and your spouse, too, for that matter, need to be built up by your words. When someone tells us verbally or writes us a note letting us know we are special to them, it can change our day, year, and even our life. All of us can remember a time when we were in a rough place and someone said something nice to us or about us, and it changed us. As parents, our children need us to be those people. Let your children have lots of memories of you letting them know the various ways you believed in them and encouraged them to have a great life.

4. **Act on every impulse you have to value them.** I remember working with a wife who was on the verge of leaving her husband and family because she never heard her husband or children say they appreciated her. She felt very undervalued and disrespected. I talked with the husband and asked him how his marriage was going. He said it was terrific. He was so in love with his wife! I asked him if he had ever told his wife how much he loved her. "No. She knows," he replied. I responded that he might want to start telling her. He did and it kept them together and growing their marriage. The same dynamic goes on with the kids. They don't know you think well of them if you don't tell them.

I began to act on every impulse to praise or compliment my kids. If I think of a positive thought about my wife or my girls, I tell them, call them, text them, or communicate it to them. It doesn't matter what time of the day it is. They never seem to think I am bothering them whenever I'm telling them I noticed or remembered something positive about them.

5. **Spend regular time with them.** One of the ways we communicate value is spending time with the other person. As adults, we can think of lots of productive, fun, or exciting ways to spend our time, and our children often lose out to these ideas. But if we are going to develop an enjoyable and encouraging family, we will have to be the one to sacrifice some of our exciting opportunities to express the value of our children. We had a rule in our home that I would spend four nights a week at home instead of teaching or pastoring others. I wanted to communicate how valuable the kids and my wife were to me. I was allowed to be out changing the world three nights a week, but the other four nights I needed to be home. Each week when the girls were small, I would take them on a date. Just that girl and me doing something out of the house together. We would go to the park. We would go to the mall. We would go to a movie. We would ride bikes or fly a kite. Whatever it was, we did something that was memorable for that child.

6. **Hug, hold, wrestle, and touch them.** Some people grew up in families that weren't hugging families. Neither my wife nor I did, but we wanted to make sure our children received value, respect, and honor in every way we could give it to them, so we learned to hug and touch. We all need appropriate loving touch. Touch communicates so much about value, importance, and significance. Use this means of communication and it will almost invisibly fill up your children. Hold your children, hug your children, wrestle with them, and put a gentle hand upon them to let them know you care and are thinking of them. Many people in our society are starving for a loving touch—don't let it be your children.

7. **Be excited to see them every time.** When my oldest daughter started driving, she started to feel like her arrival at home was unnoticed, which made her feel unwelcome, so my wife and I changed what we did when our girls came home. We would go to the garage and cheer their arrival every time. We would stop everything we were doing and stand there, welcoming them home. This may be a silly way we communicated their value, but it helped. We all have watched what happens when another person sees someone who is valuable to them. Their eyes light up or they notice them in some way. Our children are watching us to see if when we catch a glimpse

of them, do we react in an excited or noticeable way? This is a choice we can make as parents. We can change the narrative in our children's life because they see the small things that tell them they are valuable.

8. **Tell them you like them as a person.** I can remember working with a young mom and dad who were being driven crazy by the behavior of their middle school daughter. The parents were doing everything they could to communicate their love and their encouragement. I talked with the young lady and eventually she blurted out, "But they won't say that they like me!" It all clicked when mom said that. In her world, love is expected from parents, but "liking" someone is much more powerful than love. She wanted to know if her parents liked her, meaning did they like being around her? Did they like anything she was doing? When the parents began to communicate that they not only loved her but they liked her, it made a huge difference.

9. **When your child is ready to talk, be willing to listen to her stories, problems, interests, adventures, fears, and joys.** One of the things that children and teenagers want is for their parents to really listen to them. They think, "Don't react to what I am saying but really listen to what I am thinking or wondering about." It is very difficult for many parents to listen to a story when you know where it is going and what the child will want to do. But listening is saying, "I love you," "I respect you," in a way the child can receive.

   I found that my children most often wanted to talk with me after their bedtime, and yes, I knew it was so they could stay up later. But in the interest of building a relationship with them, I went along with it. They would tell me about their day at a deeper level than they would have earlier in the evening or morning. I found this time to be so valuable that I actually started rearranging my schedule so I could be alert and functional from 11:00 p.m. to 1:00 a.m. If my girls wanted to talk, I was available. I am happy to say that we solved a lot of the real problems in their life during those late-night chats. Many parents of boys tell me their sons are more open to talking when they are doing a sport or something else, side-by-side with a parent. Find the way and time that your children will feel safe to open up. Don't react to what they are saying, or they will shut down. I found myself saying, many times, "Now, that is an interesting idea. Help me understand more about that."

10. **Don't interrupt them or discount their ideas, feelings, or thoughts.** It can be so hard to hear the whole of what a child is saying on many different levels, but it is essential to let them talk it out. If we interrupt when they

are talking and hi-jack the conversation in the direction we want, they will stop talking. If we do that a few times, they will conclude their parent is not a safe person to talk to. You want to be their safe person, believe me.

They may begin telling you about how great it was to be with some group of people because Suzy or Mike was there, or they inadvertently say that someone was driving ninety miles an hour, or someone drank some vodka. Don't freak out about the girl or boy that was there, the ninety miles an hour, or the vodka. *Keep listening.* Make a mental note to yourself that you will find out more about that later. Listen to the topic and theme your child wants to talk about. Don't forget the other details, but do your best to not react to the side issue in the midst of the conversation. You can damage the relationship if you do so regularly.

11. **Do stuff they like to do.** Another way you can demonstrate value to your children is by doing some of the things they like doing. You do not need to do everything they like doing, but it is helpful if they see you trying to enter their world occasionally and valuing what they find so fascinating. If they like ice skating, then go ice skating with them. If they like video games, then play some video games with them. Realize your children want to spend time with you, that is, unless you have devalued them. They are looking for ways to have you around. What they think of first is including you in stuff they find interesting and compelling. Take it as a compliment when they want you to play board games with them or watch them do a trick or move.

My daughters loved to bounce on the trampoline. They came to me and asked if I would watch them. They always tended to ask right when I got comfortable in my easy chair, writing, checking emails, or researching things. "Will you watch me, daddy?" "Absolutely," I replied, and I would get up for five minutes and watch them on the trampoline; I wanted them to know in their soul that they are more important than my interesting and fun thing. Then they let me go back to my thing. Yes, I did have times when I was working that they could not interrupt, but I tried to let them know about those times in advance. I was not perfect on this by any stretch, but I do believe I have been able to communicate my children's deep value in a way they understood it.

12. **Do not disrespect or devalue your children in the way you discipline and train.** Unfortunately, many parents use emotional punishments rather than training and discipline. I have watched parents ground their child right before a concert or time with a friend just because they know

it will really hurt the child. Sometimes they will even say, "Maybe this will make you pay attention when I tell you something." Usually, the offense the child was guilty of is completely disconnected from the punishment. For instance, they didn't clean their room, or they were mean to their sister, and yet the discipline is aimed at the outing or the concert.

What this does is puts your child in a situation where they have to explain they have been grounded and can't do it now. They are embarrassed and devalued in the eyes of their friends. And they don't learn the lesson you want them to learn either. Instead, they learn to hate you for the emotional war you are waging against them. If your child did not clean their room, then make them clean their room and clean the rest of the house. The issue is cleanliness. If they can't get along with their sister, then have them practice getting along with their sister or have them spend extra time with the sister treating her in the right way.

Your children must always feel you are protective over their value. They have a fragile sense of self and their place in the world. They need you to constantly inject value into their soul. "You have value." "God has a plan for you." Even the way you discipline and why you discipline must reinforce their value.

13. **Do not embarrass your children.** It is very easy for parents to embarrass their children. What was cool twenty years before is no longer cool. I remember one time when my oldest was going to Youth Group at church, I volunteered to drop her off. I was too loud and boisterous, and she got embarrassed and angry with me. We had to have a whole conversation about dropping her off at Youth Group. I didn't believe I was embarrassing her, but I was. I was still her parent, but there was now a new set of rules to keep her looking good at Youth Group.

14. **Require the use of proper titles.** This does not seem like a big deal in our day and age of easy familiarity, but it is crucial that children recognize a line of respect between themselves and adults. This means that children should not call their parents by their first names. They should refer to them as Mother or Father, or Mom and Dad, or other affectionate and respectful terms referring to their parents. If the children refer to their parents by their first names, this should be corrected. There are only three people in the world who can call me "Dad."

Children should not call other adults by their first names, either, even if the adult wants them to. We found that inserting a Mr. or Ms. in front of the first name of a person who wanted to be called by their first name was sufficient to create the level of respect necessary. Without these customs of respect, children get the idea that they are equal to everyone and they do not need to conform their behavior or speech to anyone else. As a child grows up, if they have the idea that everybody is equal to them, then when they are teenagers, they will feel that they should be able to do whatever they feel like doing. They become the "gods" of their own world and we don't want that. Assigning titles of respect is one less check against rebellious independence. Proper titles and respectful usage of names is a subtle, but constant, reminder of the difference between an adult and a child.

15. **Focus on what your children are good at.** It is your job to help your child uncover the hidden talents and skills that God has woven into their life. They may not be interested in what you are interested in. They may not be the best at anything, but they have been wired to enjoy, be gifted at, and interested in a number of things, and they need you to help them find out what they are. Keep exploring hobbies, subjects, skills, talents, and interests until you find things your children are good at and interested in.

In effect, you as their parents are the ultimate guidance counselor for them. They constantly ask the questions, "What is my place in the world?" "What am I good at?" "How do I fit in?" "What is my contribution?" They do not have enough experience in the world to answer those questions accurately. They need you to help them explore new interests, talents, and skills. They may not be super grateful for your willingness to sacrifice your time, energy, and resources for their destiny, but when you help them find what they are good at, it pays off with a content child full of meaning and purpose.

Instilling Respect in Teens

I felt it was necessary to explain how respect works differently with older children and teenagers, because this seems to be a huge area of conflict within many families I talk to. The consistent testimony of Scripture is that children should honor their parents. The word honor is the word *timao* in the Greek, which means "to value." A child is to value their parents. What this valuing looks like is different as the child grows older. It begins with obedience. When a child is small, the most honorable thing a child can do is to obey their parents. When they reach the teen years or the tween years, the most honorable or valuable thing a child can do is respect their parents. Remember, respecting someone is acknowledging their value.

As a child grows, he or she is trying to establish their own independent self within the web of relationships that is their life. It is natural for a child to devalue their parents as they try and assert their independence. This natural tendency damages the child, the parent, and the family structure, as well as the society or community they live in. The child must be given room to grow toward independence while at the same time maintaining their respect for their parents. Using proper titles, addressing parents in a submissive, gentle tone, not talking back, seeking their parents' wisdom, sharing what is really happening in their life—all of these are ways that teens can honor their parents. All of these are largely controlled by the parents' behavior toward the teen. The teen is still too much a product of their emotions to reason the correct behaviors out, so they react to the environment and interactions with their parents. Parents can control whether they receive honor from their children as they become teens.

The parents' role begins to switch in the teen years. Oftentimes, parents who have done a good job of controlling their children up through the elementary grades, find that the old ways of dealing with their children do not work. This is because most children want and need different types of interactions with their parents. They need more guidance and less micro-management. They need room to be able to fail without judgment and condemnation. They need listening without reaction. They need some room to discover life as it really is with its consequences, rewards, and joys.

Instead of the desire to protect the child from every danger and solving their problems for them, parenting becomes a process of causing the child to think through the dangers on their own and make their own decisions as to what is safe and prudent.

The power of a strong, controlling parent is welcome and comforting when the child is young, but it can be smothering and destructive when the child needs to be learning how to make his or her own decisions. If the parent makes all of the child's decisions through the teen years, then the child has learned a level of dependence that is not healthy.

I have listed some tried and true ways to help your teenager become an independent and enjoyable young adult.

1. **Help your teenagers think out loud with you so they come to the right conclusion.** When your child comes to you and says they would like to do something or go somewhere, your response needs to be one of, "Let's have a discussion," rather than just rendering a verdict on the idea. You must begin to help the young person think out loud.

I can remember when my oldest and most adventuresome child asked me if she could go on a road trip with some friends. I could see why my daughter thought it was a fun possibility but she saw none of the safety, financial, or difficult issues. Rather than tell her she couldn't go, I told her it was an interesting possibility and understood how fun it could be. I asked her to help me evaluate it and also come up with a number of other possibilities that would accomplish the same goal of having fun with friends on a road trip. As my daughter did the research and looked at various elements of the trip, it became apparent to her that it was a bad idea and some of the other trips with her friends were better options. After a number of discussions, I asked her which one she thought was the wiser way to have fun with friends on a road trip and she ended up choosing the one I would have chosen. But the key is, *she* chose it. I never told her she couldn't go on the first one she proposed; I just helped her think it through. This is our new role as parents of teens and young adults.

2. **Let your teens take risks and fail in some areas so they can learn.** While they are still in your home, it is important to give your children the chance to both really fail and succeed. You want them to feel what failure feels like in a limited way so that it is not completely devastating when it comes later. They need to realize they can recover from a bad test grade, from performing poorly, from a bad personal interaction, a small car wreck, and so forth.

   Parents who insulate their children from all danger are not doing them any favors. They are really crippling their children for the future. Find little choices your children can really grapple with and even possibly fail at so they can learn from them. Let them not study sometime and see how the bad grade feels when they get it. Let them eat too much sweets or something that will give them an upset stomach. You want them to experience the direct consequences from their choices.

   Obviously, you are still protecting them from the big dangers that can wreck their life. But as they grow older, you even let them in on those processes as they will have to start protecting themselves. Do not rescue your child from every situation they have gotten themselves into. Let them feel the consequences of the real world while they are still in a safe environment.

3. **Create a small funnel at the beginning and open it up later.** One of the key ideas I was presented with when I became a parent was the funnel concept. A funnel is small on one end and gradually gets bigger until it is

very large. One of my mentors told me that this is what parenting should be like.

When your children are small, your rules and routines are very restrictive and need to open up as the children grow older. What often happens is that parents have very few rules when the children are small and then they get very restrictive when the children are older and can make really bad choices. This usually produces rebellion. Teenagers need to be given increasing freedom to make their own choices and see how these play out. They should understand that the more responsibly they act, the more freedom they will be given. If they make a series of bad choices, then the boundaries come in to protect them and the family. (See more about this in the Rules chapter.)

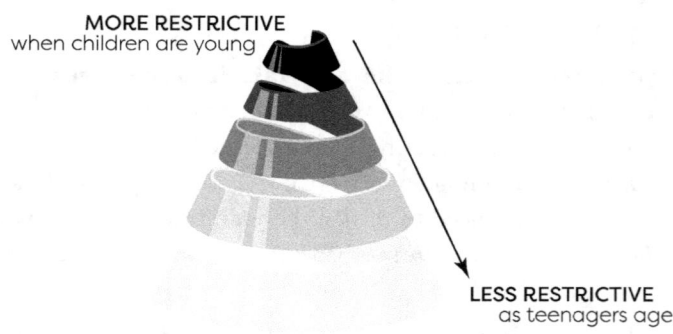

HEALTHY TEENS/ADULTS

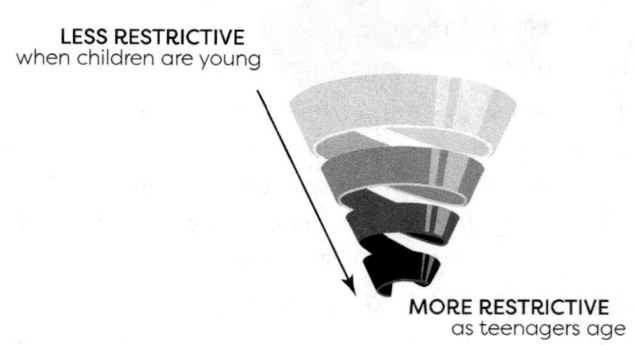

REBELLIOUS TEENS/ADULTS

4. **Block social media, TV, movies, magazines, games, phones, and books when the kids are small, and only let the boundaries move with good behavior.** It is often assumed in our world that children have the right at a very young age to participate in every form of social media, TV, movies, video games, and so forth, but this is nonsense. If something would be destructive to my children, then I have the right to restrict my children's access to it. In just the same way as a child with a severe food allergy has significant food restrictions imposed by their parents, so should immoral, illegal, and influential content be screened out until the child can handle it, or completely banned if they cannot. It is possible for a parent to be too controlling and too protective, but many children are bullied, tempted, abused, manipulated, and coerced through these various materials. Just because the other kids get to view it does not mean your children can or should.

Each request to use one of these things should lead to a discussion of real reasons and real interactions with your children. When your children realize you are not just being old fashioned or anti-everything, your family is making serious progress. And yes, you must reserve the right to pull something back if it is causing significant disruption to school work, sibling interaction, the parental relationship, chores, good friendships, physical activity, and the like. There are things your children and you should not be exposed to; therefore, it is appropriate to have blocks, restrictions, filters, and controls. It is okay to be too restrictive at first as you find the right balance for the child's growth and development.

Conclusion

The goal we are aiming for is to develop your family to be one that is pleasant and enjoyable with kids who grow into thriving, respectful, and contributing adults. Emotionally healthy kids are shielded from aspects of the world when they are not ready for them and taught to understand these influences when they can truly grasp both the benefits and the consequences of these forms of information. This process of growing your children into responsible adults requires hundreds of discussions, plans, restrictions, and interactions.

God often allows these issues to force dialogue between parents and their children. Help your children realize you love them and are taking the long view for their happiness. There are things that are more important than being popular in middle school. There are life issues that require their focus in the teen years to set them up for a great life later.

> "And may the Lord our God show us his approval and make our efforts successful. Yes, make our efforts successful!"
>
> —Psalm 90:17 nlt

Questions to Ask at the Weekly Staff Meeting:

- Do the children feel valued?
- Are our children respecting us and other adults?
- Are we valuing them enough?
- What have the kids done right in the last week?
- How have we praised them or how will we praise them?
- Are there areas of disrespect that need to be addressed with one of the children? Toys, adults, sassing, rebellion, siblings, and so forth…

3.
resources

When I first recognized that supplying resources to my children was a key component of raising them wisely, I mainly looked at financial resources. But then I came to understand there are other resources of equal if not greater significance that may allow them to really soar into their future. Without these key resources, they might never quite achieve lift off or reach their full potential.

Ephesians 6:4 (KJV) says, "And, ye fathers, provoke not your children to wrath: but bring them up in the nurture and admonition of the Lord." The idea of "the nurture of the Lord" is to supply your children with the nutrients, environment, and materials needed for them to flourish. In some ways, people are like plants that need specific nutrients to develop maximally. Your children are given eighteen years in your care to do this. Like a gardener who cares for a prized plant, you as their parent supply the fertilizer, the sunlight, the water, maybe even a greenhouse, some weeding and pruning, plus all the other things they need to prepare them for the outside world. When kids are on their own, they need to be prepared to handle the pressures life will throw at them and still make a positive contribution. This crucial issue of supplying the resources children need requires thinking, exploring, and trying things that maybe your parents did not supply for you. It is at the core of a parent's responsibility.

In our day and age, it is common to talk about under-resourced children. Usually this means financially under-resourced, but there are many resources a child needs that are far more important than just money. Each week that rolls by in a child's life are crucial for the inflow of specific resources. We know there are at least eight essential resources that allow a young boy or a young girl to really become all they can be. In Dr. Ruby Payne's book, *A Framework for Understanding Poverty*, she defines poverty as "the extent to which an individual does without resources."[2] She lists the eight key resources that affect a person's level of poverty, and I have chosen to focus on these eight here because of their demonstrated power in the lives of children. There may be other resources, but these eight are the most significant in my opinion. If children are deprived of these resources, they will be significantly hindered in life.

What resources are needed for each child to thrive and grow into a responsible adult in eighteen years' time? They are wisdom, finances, emotional, mental, spiritual, physical, support systems, and role models and mentors. I will walk through each of these resources with a fuller explanation and examples in the paragraphs below.

I have found it helpful to regularly review these eight key resources and think through how much of each should be introduced during that week to help the child grow and develop. Just as we have with all the other R's, my wife and I examined each child each week and the possibility that one of the R's is the one that needed attention for that week. Here's what that table looks like:

Resources	Dad	Mom	Child 1	Child 2	Child 3
Wisdom, Understanding and Prudence					
Financial					
Emotional					
Mental					
Spiritual					
Physical					
Support Systems					
Role Models/Mentors					

In our weekly staff meetings, we would ask, "What resources do the kids need this week that we are not thinking about or we're not aware of?" This started a discussion about the various resources we needed to pay attention to.

Wisdom, Understanding, Prudence

> "Train up a child in the way he *should* go, even when he is old he will not depart from it."
>
> —Proverbs 22:6 *(emphasis mine)*

Every child needs wisdom about who they are and how the world works. God has a S.H.A.P.E. that He has designed into every person; that is, a combination of Spiritual Gifts, Heart, Abilities, Personality, and Experiences—the prescription of who they are and what they should do in the world.[3] This information is vital for your children to know about themselves as they grow into adulthood.

I have been amazed and delighted with how helpful this information is to teenagers and young adults. It can also be life-changing to adults who feel like they are stuck in a job or career that is really not them. Look at what the scriptures say about this idea. Proverbs 22:6 is clearly a message of morality, but there is also an admonition to find out about who the child is. Some children were meant to pursue more abstract, intellectual pursuits, and others were meant to build real, concrete things and design things. The way a child should go is about morality but also what that child is created to do.

God designed us to be a specific kind of human doing specific types of things to bring hope, light, love, and joy into our world. It's our job as parents to help our children figure this out as they grow and mature.

I was very encouraged to read about the specifics of brain development in the book, *Now Discover Your Strengths*, by Marcus Buckingham and Donald Clifton. This is an excerpt about where we get our specific strengths and weaknesses. It is very instructive.

> The brain is an odd organ in that it seems to grow backwards…Your liver, your kidneys, and thankfully your skin all start small and become gradually larger until they reach the appropriate adult size. With your brain, the opposite happens. Your brain gets very big very quickly and then shrinks and shrinks into adulthood.

Sixty days before you were born your neurons start trying to communicate with one another. Each neuron reaches out – literally "reaches out" a strand called an axon—and attempts to make a connection... In fact, by the age of three, each of your hundred billion neurons has formed fifteen thousand synaptic connections for each of your hundred billion neurons.

But then something strange happens.

Between the ages of three and fifteen you lose billions and billions of these carefully forged synaptic connections. By the time you wake up on your sixteenth birthday half of your network is gone. Nature forces you to shut down billions of connections precisely so that you can be freed up to exploit the ones remaining.

To make sense of your world you will have to shut out some of this noise in your head.

Your genetic inheritance and early childhood experiences assist you in finding some connections... easier to use than others (i.e., the competitive connection, mirror neurons and swimming)....You are drawn to these connections time and time again until they become tighter and tighter. To use an internet analogy, they are your superfast T1 lines (5G). Here the signals are loud and strong.

Meanwhile, ignored and unused, other connections in parts of your network wither away. No signal at all can be heard... you may lose your center of attention connection. ... your brain freezes when you feel the eyes of the audience on you. Or perhaps you have no connection for empathy. Rationally, you understand empathy is important, but moment by moment you just can't seem to pick up the signals that other people are sending.

If nature did not whittle down your network to a smaller number of strongly forged connections, you would never become an adult. You would remain a permanent child, frozen in sensory overload.[4]

When I am coaching a leader to help them reach their full potential, I will often give them a number of different tests or assessments that show how they are wired and how to take advantage of that unique wiring. I use various tests and insights to help them see how they are different and wonderfully made for their purpose. Some of these tests include:

- Male vs. Female differences
- Myers–Briggs
- DISC TEST / Ancient Temperaments
- Love Languages
- Spiritual Gifts
- Natural Abilities
- Strengths Finders
- Eye–Memory Patterns
- Socio-Economic Hidden Rules and Background
- Family of Origin and Cultural Programming

As your children grow, you will want to expose them to these types of tests and insights so they can identify and use all that God has put within them. Each test provides a sliver, a snapshot, of who we are. None of them represent all we are, and they should not be used to put us into a box. But they should be used to identify and declare our strengths. You can find more about each of these in appendix 1.

When our children were in their teenage years, Dana and I took them to the Johnson O'Connor Research Laboratories in San Francisco to have them tested for their natural aptitudes. It was a wonderful revelation for them and for us as their parents. It is a two-and-a-half-day process where the children were actually given tests to determine how talented they were at nineteen different natural abilities. These aptitudes were compared with over eighty years of data, ranking them in terms of their aptitudes. Then we were shown what careers people with these aptitudes did the best in. It was wonderful. We discovered one of our daughters was right to want to become a scientist. One of our daughters had hidden artistic abilities we did not know about. It was very instructive and helpful for us as parents to know what way they should go. If you have an interest in this kind of aptitude testing, visit sf@jocrf.org.

I have found giving these bits of wisdom to our children act like powerful resources they can draw from throughout their life. It is often these wisdom resources that allow a child to reach their full potential as they move through life.

Financial Resources

This resource is about understanding the rules of money. One of the basic issues in a child's life is food, shelter, clothing, and the essentials needed to maintain life. These depend on whether the parents have adequate financial resources to provide them. The child is completely dependent upon the parents or guardians to supply financial resources at least throughout adolescence. Under this category, a parent should ask, *Does the child have what they need to grow and develop? Do they need new shoes? More food? Winter clothes? A new bed? Money for a school outing? An allowance?* In other words, does this child need money or something that money can buy?

I can remember when my girls were growing up, we had to keep track of the new clothes they needed as they grew. We saved money for the outings and expenses at their school and for the sports teams they were a part of. What are the financial needs of your children this week? What needs are coming up? Will they need a dress for a special dance or new sports equipment?

My girls were big into swimming. We knew they needed money to register for the sport and new swimsuits and goggles each year. There were also trips to swim meets and the expenses of meals we had to save up for.

There might even be a need for mentoring, counseling, coaching, or special clinics, which also cost money. As parents, think through the various things that would help your children and be willing to explore how you could help your children move forward regardless of cost. It's important for your child to see you sacrifice and come up with creative ways to afford things. There are usually free programs or scholarships available for those who can't afford these resources, which is also good for them to know. Be creative!

Emotional Resources

Your children have to be able to choose their responses to situations that come up in life, particularly negative ones, without becoming involved in self-destructive behavior. It means teaching them to understand the value of stamina, choices, and the rules of emotions.

Each child must be given the emotional resources to deal with stressful situations without moving into self-destructive patterns to cope with stress. As each child's needs are projected during the week, sometimes it is the emotional issues that are the most critical for that child that week. Are they facing a bully somewhere in their life? Are they dealing with disappointment? Are they exploring a new emotion (love, hate, fear, power, popularity)? Have they been given the tools to know how to deal with what they are feeling?

Kids are faced with all sorts of emotional situations and responses each day, and they need to know the answers and processes to deal with them properly. They have to figure out how to interact with all the people they will encounter in their life. If they are left to their own devices, they may discover a destructive way of dealing with a situation or person, like fighting or doing drugs, cutting themselves, and so forth. If a child can be given the appropriate emotional resources to deal with what they are feeling and what others are aiming at them, it goes a long way toward helping the child develop their full potential.

Listening is one of the most important emotional resources you can provide. Kids are young people reacting to and feeling emotions for the first time and facing choices and issues that are perplexing to them. The fact that you would listen to them is huge. I have found it very helpful when parents can set aside their parental-reaction factor during the first time you listen to a child's situation. Children will stop sharing with their parents if their parents get angry, impulsive, or demanding when they openly talk about what they are thinking and feeling. Become an emotional resource to your children by listening without judgment to what they are facing and what they are feeling. There will be time later to have a discussion about the issues at stake.

Your children also need examples of what happens when a person chooses certain actions as opposed to others. Parents usually just assume that children know what is right and wrong, but children need to understand that certain choices have significant results. These real examples are emotional resources that can help the child choose wisely. Taking children to serve at a rescue mission can help, especially if you ask the question, "What do you think led this person to being here?" Have discussions with your children about teens they know who made the decision to have sex with their boyfriend or girlfriend, or who made the decision to hide their pain through alcohol or drugs, or who acted on their desire for revenge. This is so helpful.

Many children think they don't have a choice about whether they can act upon their impulses or not. Having the emotional resources to know that they can feel something but not let it control them is huge. They don't have to give in to their emotions.

Mental Resources

Children also need the mental resources and abilities (reading, writing, computing) to think clearly about daily life. This involves helping them find where, how, and what their mind wants to learn. Every child will eventually enter the world around them, not just their parents' home. They need basic mental skills to succeed in the world at large, like common sense, as well as reading, writing, math, or computing skills. It is when they are children when these basic facts and skills should be acquired. At various times, they will likely struggle with each of these. That's ok—it's normal.

I can remember practicing reading, grammar rules, and multiplication tables with each of my children. We hired tutors at various points through their growing up because they needed to have these skills down. One of our girls was in a school for a period of time that did not stress the importance of basic math and writing skills. We, as parents, did not understand this deficit until we put her in another school and she was incredibly behind the other children her age. We put a lot of time, effort, and money to build up these crucial skills because we could not leave her without them.

Each week, parents need to ask whether the mental resources needed for that child are being poured into him or her. We changed schools, tutors, and homework amounts to make sure we gave our children the best chance to be their best self. Math is a subject that needs lots of attention for many children. It may not be all that interesting to them, or it just doesn't make sense as it is presented. Our children did not interact with math easily in elementary and high school but they are now doing very demanding jobs as adults that require math and science backgrounds. I want to believe that our patience and investigation to find the teachers, tutors, instructors, motivation, and rewards so they could stay at it helped expand their mental resources to be able to succeed at the level they are at now.

Spiritual Resources

Spiritual resources tap into a sense of purpose and guidance as children begin to understand the spiritual rules of life and how to access spiritual help.

> "The fear of the Lord is the beginning of wisdom."
>
> —Proverbs 9:10

Life has spiritual rules, like there is a God who loves them, and you reap what you sow. Children need to know how to navigate the real world in a way that reflect these rules. Giving our children a spiritual heritage that connects with God is important, so they need to see us as adults connecting with God too. We prayed with our children each night before they went to bed. When they became teenagers, we showed them how to have their own spiritual connection with God. When we faced decisions as a family, we would gather around an ottoman in the living room to ask God for wisdom and guidance. Our children saw both parents pursue the Lord personally. At dinner, we talked about what God was teaching us and guiding us to do. We took our children to church and worshipped with them as a family.

Each child needs parents who will give them every opportunity to have a real faith to guide them the rest of their life. At the weekly meeting, ask if each individual child is getting enough connection to God or if they need more. I remember one of our girls had a significant period of night terrors, so I spent extra time teaching her to pray each evening, and then prayed with her until she mastered the fears that were terrifying her. It was a spiritual issue, so we added spiritual resources until she could handle further occurrences on her own.

Another powerful spiritual resource and one that regularly needs to be explored is God's design for their life and whether they are aimed at it or not. Children need to know, "I have a purpose because God said so." Meaning and significance comes when we are connected to the infinite reference point of God. Help your children wrestle with the life of faith. What does it mean to trust God? What do they do when God does not answer prayer the way they want? How can they sense God's presence when they feel alone? What does it mean to let God guide them? All of these questions and answers are a part of the spiritual resources that children need.

Some of the most precious times in all of parenting is praying with your children at night. So many things can be discussed and prayed about. It is such a bonding time for parents, children, and God. Don't miss them!

Our family also had many interesting discussions at the dinner table. We used our family placemats to launch from a Scripture verse and then we would go off to a practical discussion of a situation that one of the children was facing at school or with friends. What are some ideas you have for your family?

Physical Resources

Physical resources consist of health, safety, mobility, and understanding the rules about them. There are times when a parent needs to look more closely at the physical resources in a child's life depending on their growth, development, or stage. Examine their room, their school, their way home, their friends, and so on. Is this boy going through puberty? Is a young lady beginning menstruation? Does a particular child need a bigger bed or a new pair of shoes? Does this child need to start the process of getting a driver's license? Do you need to find a safer way to get your child to and from school? Does your child need to be trained on stranger danger? How about romance? Are they burning the candle at both ends or signing up for too much? Are they physically safe in all the spaces where they regularly go? Many parents deal with this issue on a "feel" or "sense" basis, but it can be very helpful to have it as part of the checking process.

I can remember when our girls went through the various phases of development and I needed to recognize that they were changing and needed the physical resources to deal with their changing bodies. I can remember when we had to buy the girls mace to go on their key chains and show them how to use it. That was a very sobering day in the life of each girl and mine as their father. There will be hundreds of these types of physical resources your children will need. Keeping your eyes and ears open will help you find out about them or stumble across them. Be open to learn and be willing to be surprised. Many parents really like the age their kids are at now and don't want them to grow up. But they do, regardless of how we feel about it, so we need to adjust to that new phase. Every age bracket of my girls' lives was wonderful and enjoyable, but it was always surprising. It seemed like I had just figured out one phase, and they were on to the next one.

Support Systems

Do your children have other support systems beyond you, their parents? Do they have friends they can count on, family, neighbors, church, state, charities, and other available resources in a time of need? What is the safety net the child can count on? I can remember when my father walked me down to a neighbor who we had visited many times before and sat me down with this family friend. He said to me, "Son, if you ever need to talk or need help and you can't find me or don't want to talk to me, I want you to know you can talk to Mr. Brown here." Children need to know who they can trust beyond just their parents.

I can remember walking to the church as a very young boy when my parents were having a fight. Somehow, I knew going to the church would get me help and I would be okay. You should point out who the trustworthy organizations and trustworthy people are, so your kids don't have to try and find out for themselves. You will also need to point out who not to trust. Everyone needs to know what the safety net around them looks like.

It is a very scary thing to feel completely alone. I can remember telling one of my girls after she was in a car accident, "There is a system for everything. We are now going to access the system for dealing with a broken car. You didn't know that there was this system, but there is. There are a number of crooks in this system, but we have found these particular people and organizations to be very helpful."

Just as I pointed out to my daughters, there are systems for everything, and there are good people in each system and corrupt people in every system. They should know from you who to trust at school, at church, in the neighborhood, with a car, with their money, with employment, with friends, and so forth. They should also know who you think they shouldn't trust in each of these areas and why.

Role Models and Mentors

Role models and mentor relationships show kids what is possible beyond their parents. Who can the child access in appropriate ways to nurture and ignite the child's dreams and not engage in self-destructive behaviors? It is important for parents to realize that while they are the primary mentors and role models for their children, they alone are not sufficient for the full development of the child. Without good role models and mentors, children cannot take strides forward. Everyone tends to operate on the principle, "If we haven't seen it, we can't do it." This is one of the key roles for mentors and role models. They allow us to believe we could be doing what they are doing. We could enjoy the life that they are enjoying.

Who are your children drawn to in terms of role models and mentors? This key observation reveals significant things about your children and how they are "wired up." It is true that advertising, movies, television, and the like glorifies certain careers and certain individuals, but we can help our children see past these shallow role models.

There will be times when your children cannot receive information from you because they need to be independent of you. It is in those times when role models and mentors you select will play a crucial role. They need to be able to say what you would say but outside of your authority structure. I can remember hiring tutors, music teachers, sports coaches, connecting my girls to particular youth leaders at church, sending them to camps, conferences, seminars, and retreats so they could meet great role models. These people gave them pictures of their future, glimpses of what they could be if they worked hard and did things right. My wife and I would discuss when, who, and how to connect our children to great role models. If I found someone who was five to ten years older than my girls and I thought they would be a great role model, I would find a way to get that person to influence my child's life.

Conclusion

Caring parents want to help their children do well and go higher than they did. This can take the form of giving funds for college or some money for a down payment for a home. It can take the form of a coach or role model who is better suited to the child's interests than the parent. It can be a clear explanation of the socio-economic rules which exist across cultures. It can be listening and/or emotional counseling. It could include treatment for diseases or an ailment. Sometimes it is helping them through addiction issues. Sometimes it is just being there and having a relationship with them even when it is easier to distance yourself. Sometimes it is forcing your children to face the facts of their actions and words through treatment, interventions, and/or cutting off support until something changes. Work together to figure out which resources each child needs each week, then follow through consistently for the results you desire. It will be worth it—trust me.

Questions to Ask at the Weekly Staff Meeting:

- What resources will each child need this week?
- Are there additional resources they need in order to do exceptionally well this next week?
- What challenge is each child facing—emotionally, physically, financially, and so forth?
- What resources would unlock more of this child's talents, abilities, and future?
- Who could be a great role model for this child?

4.
rules

Recently, an exasperated young mother asked me how to get her three-year-old to mind her. Her look told the story—she was at her whit's end; she needed help. I didn't hesitate to share with her the Six R's, the most effective training methods I know of that work on children of almost any age. They were tried and true when my wife and I raised our three girls, and I was confident they would work for her child, too. A week later, that same young mother reported that these methods worked much better than she expected. She was overjoyed that she now had some tools that actually worked—and new hope for her many parenting years ahead.

"Rules" is the next of the Six R's, the expectations, guardrails, boundaries, and guidelines as set by both the Great Commandments (Matt. 22:37–39) and the Ten Commandments (Ex. 20:1–17). The key to whether you have an enjoyable family or hell on earth is your willingness to teach these rules to your kids over and over again, without tiring of the telling, teaching, training, retelling, reteaching, and retraining…it can be exhausting, I know, but the rewards are worth it.

I find in my counseling and pastoral duties that parents are truly amazed their children don't know how they are expected to behave. Afterall, isn't is enough to tell them once? Shouldn't they be able to remember? No, one time isn't enough. It takes about eighteen years of consistent and adaptable instruction to make it all stick.

I believe the scriptures tell us over and over again that the joy of parenting is about getting the information you know into your children so they can live a loving and successful life, even more successful than the one you have lived. Psalm 19:7–8 says,

> "The law of the Lord is perfect, restoring the soul; The testimony of the Lord is sure, making wise the simple.
>
> The precepts of the Lord are right, rejoicing the heart; The commandment of the Lord is pure, enlightening the eyes."

Deuteronomy 6:6–9 outlines a parent's duty to the fullest extent:

> "These words, which I am commanding you today, shall be on your heart. You shall teach them diligently to your sons and shall talk of them when you sit in your house and when you walk by the way and when you lie down and when you rise up. You shall bind them as a sign on your hand and they shall be as frontals on your forehead. You shall write them on the doorposts of your house and on your gates."

Scripture is clear and still the most reliable source of biblical parenting advice.

One CASA Columbia University study reported on what types of parenting behaviors would move kids away from drug, tobacco, and alcohol behaviors. The design of the study was brilliant. The researchers interviewed hundreds of families. If the children of a family did not have drug or alcohol problems, they were asked about their parenting process. After collecting all of these various families' input, they cross-checked the common practices. Their findings were consistent with what you might think they would be. What they found was that if a family was willing to practice ten of twelve active parenting processes, the family would be virtually guaranteed to not have drug and alcohol problems with their children.

1. Monitoring television use.
2. Monitoring internet use.
3. Restricting music purchased, streamed, and listened to.
4. Knowing the child's whereabout at all times.
5. Being told the truth about any activity the child is involved in.
6. Awareness of and deep interest in the child's academic performance.
7. A curfew was set and enforced.
8. An adult was home when the child came home from school.
9. The family ate dinner together six to seven nights a week.
10. The television was turned off during dinner.
11. Children were assigned and accountable for doing chores around the home.
12. There is a predetermined, known response to substance abuse: extreme anger and consequences.

These active parenting processes produced amazing results, each ensuring the success of the children's future against alcohol, tobacco, and drug abuse. Which ones are you practicing, and which ones are missing from your parenting toolkit? Make a commitment to inject ten to twelve of these into your family.[5]

Training and Consistency

Your children count on you to help them figure out how to be successful and live within a loving family. It is generally true that your children want to please you and want your admiration and appreciation. (Yes, some children hate their parents but usually that is due to abuse or a mental illness or a physical disease process). Your children need love, admiration, and praise, just as you need and want loving, appreciative, well-behaved children. They want to know how to succeed at life, and you want them to succeed at life. Embrace the fact that you and your children want the same thing.

So how do you get there? Through training and consistency. Let's take a look at this from the world of man's best friend—dogs. While it is not a completely parallel world, this analogy can be very helpful. When do people enjoy their dogs the most? When the dog is behaving like the owner wants and expects. In order to have a dog that minds and does what the owner wants, it requires lots of training and consistency. The owner of the dog does not resent having to train the dog. The owner of the dog enjoys having time with the dog. This training is a way of spending time with it. The dog wants to please its owner, and the dog wants to spend time with its owner. There are people who purchase dogs and never spend time with them, never train them; they leave them in the back yard and wonder why the dog is not enjoyable to be around. It jumps up on people. It barks at the wrong time. It chews the wrong things. We have all seen people who have their dogs with them almost 24/7; the dog knows their moods and gives their owner great joy because the owner is clear about what is expected.

When you take your children to the store or to the park or to school and they make you proud of how they act, this is a reflection of how you have trained them. They learned how to act from you. They want to receive your congratulations and affection. Every time you sit down to dinner or take them out in public or send them to a friend's house, it is an opportunity for training and a test of whether they know how to behave. Every time they greet a stranger, answer the phone, or talk to other adults, it is a pop quiz on how they were trained to speak. They are doing what you trained them to do. Every time they face a disappointment or a time of elation or "No, you can't do that," they will display what you trained them about emotional processing and control.

Yes, wise parenting is a lot of work, but it is wonderful work if you embrace it and realize it is the key to your children having a great life—the way to having an enjoyable family for many years to come. God will give you lots of opportunities to spend time with your children: homework, school shows, church presentations, bedtimes, meals, evenings, family crises, and so forth. All are opportunities to train your children by explaining what is expected, demonstrating what to say, practicing hard work, showing what should have been done even if you as the parent didn't do it.

This 24/7, wonderful gig called parenting will bring you more love, joy, meaning, and crises than almost anything you can imagine. You can throw yourself into it and have a wonderful life, or you can ignore the needs for instruction, training, and practice and have constant grief. Training will vary as the kids get older, but there is so much joy and love if you will be clear and repetitive about your expectations.

RULES AS EXPECTATIONS

An enjoyable family is made up of children who meet or exceed your expectations. Sounds easy, right? Well it's not. But there are four things you can do to get them there.

First, make it clear what you expect your children to do.

Second, make them practice doing this new thing.

Third, positively reward any performance of this expectation.

Fourth, negatively reward any deviation from this behavior.

Parents who express their positive and negative expectations clearly and often are the ones who have an enjoyable family. You cannot be fuzzy or vague about the way to live life, because your children will not know what to do. Your ability to be absolutely clear in terms of what needs to be done in a particular circumstance will help your children and your joy-factor abundantly. We want to believe that our children know what to do because we have told them, but they will show us by whether they do it correctly or not if we have been clear about the expectation or not.

For the expectation to really sink in, we need to reward and model and rebuke consistently. They need to know what brings consequences and rewards. I can remember a time when my wife and I were at our wits end trying to think of things to do with our kids. We were essentially trying to be fun directors and entertainers. We started to realize that we were not cruise directors for our children—we were their parents. We didn't have the ability to constantly provide fun and interesting things in their lives on a consistent basis. Someone had to be the grown up! We soon stopped trying to be the source of everything for them and helped them begin to navigate real life. Life is fun and interesting for the most part, but sometimes life is boring and you have to think up fun things yourself.

Today, there is a new type of parenting that does not train children properly at all. Parents are deferring to the television to do it; they let the public schools do it; they let the children's friends do it; they even give the church primary responsibility for spiritually training them. There are three major things wrong with this approach:

First, your children are watching what you do good or bad, right or wrong, and copying it.

Second, these other people do not always have the child's best interests at heart or cannot fulfill everything that is needed.

Third, training your children is ultimately your responsibility, and no one else's.

These methods are the antithesis of wise parenting. You are responsible for training these children of yours. But don't worry: you are uniquely equipped to raise them well. You can do it with God's help and other people in your village of support!

You are not alone.

Four Steps to Set (and Re-Set) Expectations

Setting expectations continually comes back to four steps. You will end up repeating these more than you ever thought possible but keep at it. I would suggest posting these on the refrigerator.

1.
Set the expectation.
You will make the bed.

2.
Explain the expectation.
You will take all the things off the bed.

You will pull the sheets up and tuck them in.

You will pull up the covers and tuck them in.

You will put the pillows on the bed at the head of the bed.

You will put the things that were on the bed in the closet or wherever they go in the house.

3.
Demonstrate the expectation.

Here is how you take the things off the bed.
Here is how you pull up the sheets and tuck them in.
Here is how you pull up the covers.
Here is how you place the pillows.
Here is how you put the things on the bed in the closet.

4.
Practice the expectation.

Undo all the things you just did and let them try.
Let them practice these five times.

If they don't do it correctly...

1.
Re-set the expectation.

Re-explain what you want done without anger.
They will need to hear these instructions many times.

2.
Re-explain the expectation.

They will forget what it means to do what you want or will try and shorten the amount of work involved, so show them again.

3.
Re-demonstrate the expectation.

Yes, demonstrate what you want so there is no question.

4.
Re-practice the expectation.

Make them show you that they can do what you ask.
Just because you have said it, doesn't mean they can do it.
Be patient with their learning-and-remembering curve.

Don't forget to enact consequences. (See chapter on Responsibilities.)

1.
Words Consequences

Some children will respond with explanations and gentle reminders.

2.
Actions Consequences

Some children will require that you demonstrate what is to be done.
Some will require that you make them practice the desired results.
Some children will require that you bring positive or negative incentives to their doing what you expect.

Examples of Expectations

Below are areas that children need to be trained in and require setting expectations. Address them in your Weekly Staff Meeting as they come up. Devise a training plan for how to teach each child in these areas. (More on this in the Responsibility chapter.)

- Meals
- Visiting relatives
- School work
- Friends
- Movies
- Cleanliness
- Bedtime
- After school
- Television
- Social media

- Talking to adults
- Disagreements
- Being at school
- Vacations
- Eating out
- Driving
- Music/internet/video games
- Addressing siblings
- Waking up
- Handling money
- When they make a mistake
- Being a passenger

Rules as Guardrails

In a sense, rules are like guardrails put in place to guide and guard the child in life so they don't fall off a cliff. Parents have way more real-world experiences to draw from than kids do. We have lived through our own mistakes and have felt the consequences for our actions. Kids need their parents to help them understand the natural laws of the way the world works while at the same time allowing them to feel the pain from the consequences of their own actions. It's a fine line between helping them and letting them fail for a greater lesson. Sometimes it is black and white; other times it is very gray.

Take gravity. Gravity is a law that will take effect no matter what we think. If a child walks off the top of a building, the child will fall whether they realize this will happen or not. Parents know the pitfalls of life, the things that will cause children harm even if they are unaware, like running out into the street and being struck by a car, or coming into the kitchen and pulling a pot of boiling water down on their head. The guardrails we put in place help a child learn the lesson while under your supervision and hopefully avoid a more severe fall later on.

Guardrails are designed to keep kids from harming themselves. We put safety locks on doors and childproof caps on bottles so that children can't do things they don't understand. We use car seats in cars, place screens in front of the fireplace, put fences around the yard, and lock dangerous chemicals in cabinets. We effectively put them in a bubble when they are young where the dangers and harm of the adult world are not foisted upon them. They are not designed to handle the pressures and consequences of the adult world when they are small. They need guardrails so they don't make huge mistakes before they really understand what they are doing.

This is why parents put rules on children's behavior so they can prepare them for when they go out into the "adult world" when many of the guardrails are taken off. Children will constantly test these guardrails, and eventually, they will be able to choose to ignore the guardrails as teens or adults.

Be aware that your guardrails are not the same as God's laws. Your rules point out there is something dangerous ahead on the other side of the guardrail. I have watched too many parents who instruct their children that their little rule is the all-important edict from God, so he or she is expecting something really bad to happen when they stay up too late, drink one sip of alcohol, watch an R-rated video, or kiss a person of the opposite sex. The child must begin to understand that as they grow through the teen years, the parent's rules are meant to help them understand the dangers as they approach a significant moral choice. They are meant to keep them back from the moral choice so they are not forced to face that choice when they are too young to really make a wise decision.

Guardrails are also put in place to protect a child and even an adult from violating God's laws where consequences will be enforced and life-altering decisions are made. God has told us there are certain moral laws that when violated begin to bring difficulty and consequences into our lives and the lives of those around us. They are His guardrails to us. We don't talk enough about these ideas and this is why parents do not help children understand their rules in light of the moral laws of God. These laws are given in the Ten Commandments and form the foundation of western civilization. Each one is an indicator of a win–lose line where the person, the community, and the society begins to lose if something is pursued past that line. Both you and other people are damaged when the moral laws of God are broken.

Help them think of the Ten Commandments this way:

If you want something so badly that you will elevate it over God in your life, it will damage you and others.

If you want something so badly that you will worship something that is less than God, it will damage you and others.

If you want something so badly that you will curse, swear, and verbally abuse God and others to get it, it will damage you and others.

If you want something so badly that you will violate the principle of balance between rest, work, and worship to have it, it will damage you and others.

If you want something so badly that you are willing to rebel from good authority in your life to get it, it will damage you and others.

If you want something so badly that you are willing to use the threat of violence, violence, or murder to get what you want, it will damage you and others.

If you want pleasure so badly that you are willing to be unfaithful to God and your spouse to get what you want, it will damage yourself and others.

If you want something so badly that you will steal from another person to gain it, it will damage you and others.

If you want something so badly that you are willing to lie to gain it, it will damage you and the people around you and others.

If you want something so badly that you would scheme to take someone or something another person has, it will damage you and others.

Examples of Guardrails

- Put them to bed before they want to go to sleep so they will get the rest their growing bodies need.
- Don't let them eat all the sweets they want (except maybe Halloween) so they'll grow strong and not rot their teeth.
- Don't let them watch certain television shows and movies that would expose them to immoral, violent, or adult information they cannot process at a young age.
- Don't give them alcohol when they are young because they are not ready to process the chemicals and toxins in their small little bodies.
- Make sure that the medicines you give them are designed for children and are not adult doses.
- Don't let them read anything they want just because they want to read it.
- Don't let them pick their friends and who they will spend the night with when they are young as they may not be able to fully survey the situation and its dangers.
- Make them do homework when they would rather be out playing.
- Make them participate in family time even though they would rather stay in their room and talk on the phone or do what they want at that moment.

In other words, through the use of arbitrary guardrails, parents block what the child wants when they are young so they do not harm themselves, their future, or the family. Every family has guardrails that all children don't like, but they are crucial to having an enjoyable family and for the children to grow up safe and realize their maximal potential. This imposition of guardrails into children's lives is a part of being a wise parent.

Rules as Boundaries: The Box Illustration

Rules are also boundaries that start off small and grow as they develop. When we were raising our girls, we used an illustration of a box to help them understand what was happening to them as they grew up. I put the drawings you see below on my refrigerator so that everybody in the family saw the visual explanation of the box they were in.

As their father and leader, I explained this idea of the box to them at the dinner table and again privately at various times throughout their lives. I wanted them to understand why we as a family had rules that other families did not have. And I wanted them to understand that as they grew older and were more responsible, the opportunities and choices they had would grow. Eventually, I would release them to the care of God and their own conscience to make all of their own choices. I was doing the best I could to prepare them for that day when they would grow up and leave our house and be on their own.

For me, I chose to use the illustration of a box, but you can choose a different illustration. My children understood this one clearly. I used variations of the box throughout their growing up to explain why they were getting a bigger box or a smaller box. I talked about how their older and younger siblings had different sized boxes because of their ages and behaviors. (See appendix 3.)

Lesson 1: Explain the Box

For the first box illustration, I told my girls that I loved them very much and it was my job to protect them, direct them, and provide for them. In order to live well, their mother and I made rules for their conduct, which were designed to help them live a loving and wonderful life. I explained that, yes, there were things I did not want them to do, but it was because I didn't want them to get hurt playing with things they didn't understand or were not able to really handle well yet. Their mother and I would teach them how to live a wonderful life—what to say, how to say it, how to act in various situations, and how to process and understand their emotions. I would make the box as large as possible and as safe as possible.

"Please live in the box," I asked. "When you go outside the box, we will re-explain and re-demonstrate and practice and get you to think about what

The Box

You live in the box made of my rules for your conduct.

to do."

Lesson 2: Anger and Consequences

In the next part of the box illustration, I also explained why mommy and daddy sometimes get angry at them. We said something like, "When you are consistently pushing outside the box, we will do the best we can to explain, demonstrate, practice, re-explain, and re-practice, but we will get frustrated at times when we see you not doing what we believe we have clearly explained and demonstrated. We get angry when you are outside the box in your behavior. Mommy and daddy will apologize when we have been angry with you for the wrong reason, but you can expect that we will be frustrated, irritated, and even angry with you when it is clear that you know what to do. We always love you and nothing will ever change that. We will re-explain again and practice again the right behavior, but understand when you push at edges of the box, we get irritated."

This idea really helped my girls understand where the irritation, frustration, and anger came from. It did not make them angels, but it allowed us to have much more fruitful conversations, explanations, practice sessions, and

Lesson #2 – *Anger and Consequences*

Stay in the Box

Stay inside of the commands & desires of your parents, and you will be in the joy of your mother and father.

consequences. This is the picture we had on the refrigerator for years.

Lesson 3: The Box Can Change to Be Bigger

As my children got older in the elementary years (7–11 years of age), I put up another box illustration that seemed to help them. They were making choices and getting more privileges and more opportunities with sports, friends, school, activities, and church. I wanted them to understand why this was happening. It was not just because they were growing up. It was because they were growing in their responsibility and choices. We could allow the box to grow because they were making better and better choices. I wanted them to

understand that the size of the box was up to them. This is the picture I put on the refrigerator in those years.

The phrase that I wanted them to remember was:

"When you don't know what to do, I want you to choose what you think I would do in that situation."

If my children did what they thought I would do, then I can always live with that decision. I wanted my children to know how much I loved them and how they could bring joy to our family. I was doing the best I knew how to prepare them for the decisions and choices they would face, but there would be some that I would miss. They would need to make the best choice they could in a given situation based upon what they knew about God and their parents.

Lesson 4: The Box Can Change to Be Smaller

I also wanted them to understand that just as the box can get bigger, it can get smaller. If their attitude, words, actions, or motives changed, then the box would have to get smaller so that they could feel the consequences from their choices. We were raising them to live in a cause-and-effect world where they

would need to understand the world that God had made based upon their choices and the choices of others.

Lesson 5: Living within God's Box

The final box illustration I shared with each of my girls on her eleventh birthday. I took them individually to the mall and explained the box from a different perspective. These proved to be wonderful times of interaction and anticipation of the teen years and all the fun and challenge those years would be. I would draw the boxes within boxes that you see below on a napkin, explaining that God's law is the box that their mom and dad live within. God brings consequences and training when we do not live inside His box. That is why mom and dad had a box just inside of God's box, so we did not get too close to breaking God's rules and laws. Yes, there are people who do things that we don't do, but we are trying to avoid adultery, anger, stealing, blasphemy, coveting, and the like.

I explained to my children that as they went through the teen years, their box would get larger preparing them for the time when they would have to draw their own box inside God's box. That time would most likely come when they finished college and were completely on their own. I let them know that they could draw a box outside of God's box and deal with God's consequences and

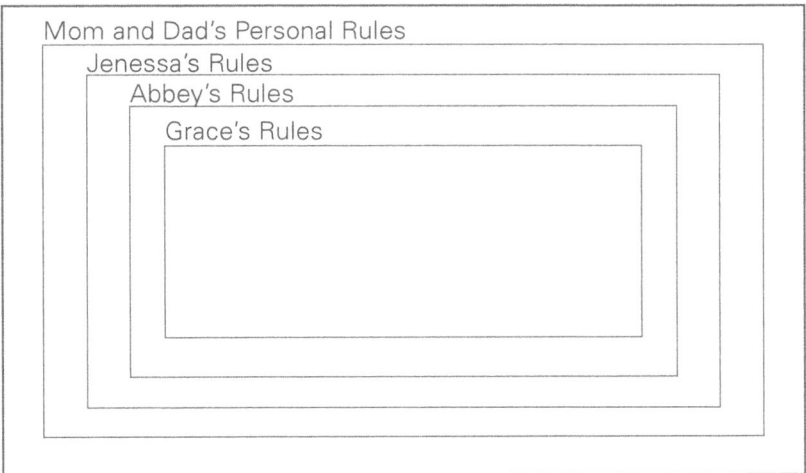

retraining, but I did not recommend it. We even talked about teenagers and adults they knew who were clearly living outside of God's box. We talked about the consequences and difficulty of those who live outside of God's box.

The older girls enjoyed the fact that their younger sister had a smaller box than they did, and the younger girls enjoyed that their box had the chance to grow significantly. I talked about various things that would come up in the teen years, such as romance, driving, new friends, college, sports, and the like, that were going to present challenges and opportunities. I wanted them to know that I was still going to love them, protect them, direct them, and encourage them, but they would have more input into the things that happened as they grew up. The same rules applied: the box can get bigger and the box can get smaller. It was all based upon their choices in five areas: words, actions, thoughts, emotions, attitude. Their teen years were going to be the best. They were going to have lots of questions and lots of new experiences, and we would face them together.

SETTING HEALTHY RULES

Wise parents want their children to be equipped to have a great life. This means knowing where the love and rewards exist and where the dangers and destruction reside. Wise parents realize that they will not always be there guiding their children, nor should they be. The children will grow into adults and will need fundamental guidelines and boundaries helping them as they live their life. The following are fourteen biblical, practical, and loving rules—the expectations, guardrails, and boundaries that parents have used over many centuries.

1. **Say the Ten Commandments or the Lord's Prayer at dinnertime.**

   Connect your children to the family rules (bedtime, going to school, no alcohol, certain shows okay and others not, respectful greetings for relatives and adults, and so forth) and to the larger moral foundation of God's laws by teaching them the Ten Commandments. This is perfect for a spiritual devotional time during dinner. I included a number of classic Judeo-Christian texts for consideration. I made placemats that were placed under the plates each evening. I wanted my children to be very familiar with the virtues, qualities, and laws that came from the Bible. (See appendix 2 for an example of the placemats we used around our dinner table.)

2. **Repeat your expectations for their behavior constantly.**

   Parents must constantly repeat what is expected of the children in various situations or they will not know to apply those rules of conduct to that situation. Right before going to school, repeat the rules of behavior for being at school. Right before going into a restaurant, repeat the rules for being in a restaurant. Right before having the evening meal, repeat the rules for having a great evening meal. It is not an accident that the great sports teams repeat and repeat what the various players need to do in the situations they will face in the game. Parenting is the same way. Your children will not remember what to do, so remind them what is expected of them; they will have a much higher rate of success in doing what you expect and you all having a great time.

3. **Quiz them about how they should behave in certain situations.**

   It is not what you say but what you emphasize. A number of years ago, I was reading an article about a football team that had a very low rate of fumbles during games. The coach was asked if they spent a lot of time teaching how not to fumble. "No," he said. "We emphasize it constantly. All running backs are required to carry a ball with them at all times and everyone at any time is encouraged to knock it out of their hands. In this way the running backs are always encouraged to keep the ball secure."

   It can be very helpful to ask the children what is expected of them in certain situations. The one who gets the answer right can receive a prize or praise. These pop quizzes are a fun way to solidify the importance of your expectations.

4. **Attach significant, but reasonable, consequences for breaking the family rules.**

   Without rewards or consequences, your child won't know if they did it right or wrong. They will need you to repeat, demonstrate, have them practice, retrain, give them incentives to do it the way you say it should be done, and bring negative consequences to them if that helps them to focus and remember better.

   The children will watch and see what happens to those who break the family rules. If there are no consequences, then the rules are not important; but if there are significant and serious consequences to breaking the rules, then keeping them becomes more important. The consequences could be time without a computer; it could be time in the room alone with no media; it could be reading aloud; it could be practicing the right way; it could be twenty-five pushups; it could be singing a song in front of the family; it could be any of the responsibility techniques discussed in the upcoming Responsibility chapter. But it must be something for the rule to exist. If there is no consequence, there is no rule.

5. **Explain how your rules protect against breaking God's law in the Ten Commandments.**

   If your family has a rule about wearing a certain type of clothing (provocative) or not saying "bad" words to each other, then it is important to occasionally help the children understand how those rules distantly connect to the Ten Commandments of no adultery and no cursing or swearing. The rules and laws have to have some kind of connection. The restrictions that your children endure must be for their safety, their moral formation, or to help others.

6. **Help them understand *why* you set the limits where you did.**

   Explain to your children in the elementary years and again in the teen years how your rules were formed. Why did you say not to watch certain movies? Why have you refrained from alcohol? Why did you have them go to bed at 8:00 p.m. and then 9:00 p.m. and now 10:00 p.m.? Why did you not let them dress up as certain characters? Why did you want them to brush their teeth every evening? As your children approach the later teen years, and as they begin to form their own guardrails and ways to keep themselves from falling victim to various temptations, they need to see how you reasoned out the rules you imposed on them.

7. **Show, talk, demonstrate, and illustrate what happens to people who violate God's rules.**

   Sometime we protect our children from the consequences of bad choices and we do not let them see what happens when people choose to spend their money unwisely or involve themselves in drug or alcohol abuse or sexual unfaithfulness. The children need to see what bad choices do to people. Yes, there is always the possibility of repentance and redemption, but poor choices have real consequences.

   I can remember pointing out as the children got into the later teen years the choices of people they knew and relatives. These examples of the negative were powerful instructors. I also used the scriptural examples of bad choices. I used to take my daughters to the mall and the airport and have them watch the eyes of the men as ladies went by them. What did their eyes do and where did they focus? This was instructive for the girls to see that many men are super-sexualized and not really focused on the face of the women. I would ask them what kind of relationship would those sexualized men have with their girlfriends and their wives?

8. **Explain that they will get to set their own box someday under God.**

   Each of your children must connect the dots between the time when they live in a box of your expected behaviors and the day when they will live in a box of God's expected behaviors. You will release them into the adult world where God will keep track of what they do and how they live. He will bless, reprove, encourage, and allow consequences to come into their life. If children think there is nothing beyond their parents or bosses or government, they will believe that if they can hide behaviors from their immediate authorities, they have gotten away with their behavior.

9. **It is okay to have adult activities, teen activities, and child activities.**

   As your children are growing up, there will need to be differences between things that adults can do that children can't do...and differences that teens can do that elementary children can't do...and things that older elementary children can do that younger children cannot do. These age, maturity, and behavior differences must exist so that the children will understand that the choices they make determine the size of the box they live in.

This also means that just because a child gets older, they should not necessarily get more privileges and opportunities. Some privileges will come because of age but not all. Some that are gained because of age can be lost because of poor choices.

10. Do not bend the rules; it is important to stay firm.

Rules can change and go away but they should not bend for just any reason. Do not bend the rules for a favorite child, or because it is more convenient to not enforce the rules this time. If a rule is important, enforce it. If it is not important, then remove it.

11. Rules build family identity.

Your children will complain about some of your rules, but it is those bedtime rules, TV rules, friend rules, homework rules, school night rules, computer rules, Christmas rules, and the like that will let your children know you are a special family who loves each other. These rules are part of what sets them apart. They need these to be special.

12. Do not set rules more lenient than the government.

One of the things that helps many parents is various government rules and guidelines: movie ratings, medicine dosage, screen time for young children, amount of sleep, healthy eating and nutrition, amount of exercise, time spent doing homework, and drinking age. Many families are stricter than the government on a number of things and they use the guidelines and rules from the broad government ideas to provide a baseline. Your children are always scanning other families to find others who allow them to do what you do not allow them to do. It can be very helpful to point to the government rules as well as your research and understanding and convictions for why your rules are where they are.

13. Let them set some of their boundaries in their teen years.

As your children grow through the teen years, it is important to let them start setting where they put the rules and guidelines. This can refer to bed times, music, dress codes, school classes, and so forth. They need to begin owning their life. If they really understand that rules are about directing their life toward their goals in life, then they should start setting some of their own guardrails.

Some of the most enjoyable discussions we had with our children was about why we set the boundaries for certain things in our lives where we did. They wanted to know why we did what we did with alcohol, why we went to bed when we did, why we didn't go to certain movies, and why we hung out with certain people and not others. All of these discussions go into the teenager's mind as they look forward to the time when they will be free of their parents' control. If the discussion is handled well and the opportunities for change are present, it is interesting how often the child will adopt the parents' rules as they get older.

14. **Ask them questions about where their boundaries will be using research. Do not assume they will automatically adopt your boundaries.**

    One of the most helpful discussions that I had with my girls is research, discussions, and interactions about where the rules should go on certain issues. What happens when children have no bedtime? What happens when children do not do their homework? What happens when teens drink alcohol? What happens when romance goes too far in the teen years? What happens when teens drive late at night? What happens when friends are in the car with a teen driver? These discussions can allow your children to look for facts and not just push for the freedoms they want.

Conclusion

One of the most important elements in raising children is setting and enforcing rules. You as parents must have them. You as parents must express them. If you are to turn your children and you into a joyful family, you must have rules. Enjoy these and help your children enjoy them and understand them. Yes, there will be times when they will not like them, but that's part of being a kid. Love your children by giving them the best opportunity to succeed in life. Train them to live a loving and productive life through what you teach them directly and who and what you expose them to. Someday, they'll look back at their childhood and realize the wisdom you used in raising them. They may even thank you for it.

Questions to Ask at the Weekly Staff Meeting:

- How are the kids doing with our rules, expectations, guardrails, and boundaries?

- Are we and they clearly understanding our expectations and boundaries?

- Do they understand the Ten Commandments? How can we teach them more effectively?
- Where are the kids doing what we expect?
- Where are they consistently not doing what we expect? Why? How to train?
- Where are the kids moving toward a danger or destruction zone?
- We cannot keep our children out of all difficulty or danger, but we can explain what is coming so they will know we knew. Where can we allow them to explore a bit more? What consequences do we need to allow them to go through?

5. routines

One secret to wise parenting is routines. A routine is a system that informs how we are to behave in certain situations. Every one of us lives based on systems we picked up from our parents or developed on our own over time. If you have the right system in place (routine), then you will be successful in that part of your life. We have hundreds of them and we don't even realize it.

Routines tell children how to do things well. If parents use them consistently and correctly, they eliminate so much anger and rebellion during the teen years. In Dana's and my case, having a routine for our kids at different stages of their lives was really helpful for us, and they thrived in them. They told us how comfortable the girls were with knowing what was expected of them in certain situations, which increased their security.

Parents don't often think about this, but they need to instill into their children all the systems they will need for healthy and successful living. It is the parents' job to teach their children routines for how to handle the things of life.

Here is how we go to bed.

Here is what we do when we wake up.

Here is how we eat dinner.

Here is how we act when at a dinner party.

Here is how we go to the bathroom.

Here is how we get ready for school or work.

Here is how we handle our money.

Here is how we greet one another.

Here is how we have a discussion when we are mad at the other person.

There are hundreds like these to teach them while they are under our roof. Lucky for us, we have eighteen to twenty years to do so.

Every interaction is a system of steps to learn. The reason why we are nervous or even fearful when we do something for the first time is because we haven't yet learned the system for handling that new assignment. Your children are the same way. So to help them overcome fears or anxiety, teach them routines and good habits. The better the routines you teach them, the easier life will be as they grow up—for you and them.

Any routines you forget to teach your children leave them not knowing what to do in certain circumstances. Ninety percent of the time when your children annoy you or irritate you it is because they are not following the routine you would prefer; instead, they are doing their own thing or following some routine of a friend of theirs, or worse, something they saw on TV. When you find your child does not know what to do, don't get mad at them—teach them the proper routine and make them practice it until they can do it.

Let me share with you three stories about routines we used in our children's lives and how important they were.

When our children were very small, I can remember one meal at a restaurant where the whole area around our table was a complete disaster when we got up to leave. It was so embarrassing! Our children had basically thrown, pushed, dropped, and discarded all kinds of food around us. It was an absolute mess. It was not the kids' fault, however; it was our fault for not training them to be careful in their eating routines. At our next weekly staff meeting, we talked about it and thought through what needed to be practiced and routinized so we could go out to eat without making such a mess. We began practicing these new actions at home until eventually the kids could eat there without making a mess. It took a while, but three months later, when we took them to a restaurant, they did not make a mess at all. The meal we had with another family was pleasant, courteous, and non-messy. They were congratulating us on how well behaved our children were. Our planning and diligence paid off.

When our children were just infants, just a few months old, we discovered two routines we needed to introduce that would make all the difference in our lives and theirs. The first one was about eating. We had a choice: we could allow our children to eat whenever they felt like it, or we could bring routine to their eating. Slowly but surely, we were able to increase the time between their bottles and they began to eat much more thoroughly and consistently. This also changed the way they slept, which was the other routine they needed. We encouraged them to nap at prescribed times and sleep longer at night. This regulated their bodies to sleep longer at night and for longer stretches during the day at nap time. These two routines helped my wife and I in tremendous ways.

At school age, we introduced them to after-school routines and homework routines that would stay with them for the rest of their lives. Like many children, they wanted to play after they got home from school and we also wanted them to unwind for a little while. But it was important to help them develop routines so they could balance resting and getting their homework done. Our new routine consisted of them talking with one of us about what happened at school, changing clothes, and doing homework. If after-school time has positive routines built in, it can be very productive both for the parents and the children. On the other hand, if it is treated as "do whatever you feel like," then the children internalize that they should be rewarded with whatever they like to do after a few hours of "work."

We saw firsthand how important routines like these were for producing joy in our family. We instigated or taught a new routine for what to do when faced with something for the first time at the various ages and stages of their growing up.

Making Routines Stick

Everything about parenting is really about teaching, training, practicing, and re-practicing positive routines. In our case, routines made us feel more prepared. We had a plan and a back-up plan if our initial plan didn't work out. It made outings so much easier. Dana really enjoyed creating the routines for our girls when they were little. She likes structure and planning, so these routines helped her because she knew what was ahead in her day and what to expect. Then she would add extra things into the day more spontaneously if she wanted to because she had a basic structure to the day and week.

Sometimes as parents we don't discover we have missed something until our children don't know what to do in a certain situation or can't remember what we taught them. This is a wonderful experience if the parent can stay positive and realize it is time for training or re-training a routine. It doesn't mean that your children are being rebellious or stupid; it means that the routine is not cemented into their way of living yet. So teach it; reteach it; have them practice it. Enjoy the process of helping your children succeed in life. Don't resent them; embrace this as the opportunity of a lifetime. Teach them patiently what they could and should be doing. It will take them hearing and practicing something dozens, maybe even hundreds, of times before they really have that routine down for that situation. Twenty years from now, your children will still be doing positive routines you taught them when they were small.

If you do routines right, then life gets very easy…your children go on auto-pilot doing helpful things for themselves and the family. Since you are the one who decides what a particular routine looks like to your young children, you can change a routine if one is not working or add something to a routine that you were not taught. It is in many of these routines that so much other teaching, training, and love can be communicated.

Now it is also true that many parents do not know what a given routine should include. That's why I have included these guidelines that will make them stick. Use these to figure out which routines to create and how to go about doing them. There are lots of ways of learning about how to do the basic routine well.

First, Strategize

We all have routines but many times we go about them without even thinking if they are all that helpful or effective. That's why it is crucial to talk about how the family is doing and what needs to be done to improve its functioning. Your weekly staff meeting is where this comes in. Discuss what is working and what is not working, then form what routine(s) each child needs to be working on right then. Since children mature and grow at different paces, chances are they aren't all going to be working on the same things at the same time, except for shared experiences, like mealtimes.

A child will let you know a new routine or a change is needed by their bad behavior, or how you are really irritated about something they are doing or not doing. You can use these as indicators that training is needed in that area. Use the weekly meeting to identify the necessary routine and plan your strategy to implement it. Check back the following week to see what progress you're noticing and make adjustments if necessary.

The weekly meeting has been one of the best routines for us as role models for our kids. We talk about things by planning ahead rather than debriefing after the fact. In our meetings when they were little, we talked about schedules, vacations, money, how each girl was doing, and what we could be working on with each. We still have meetings to this day—even though they don't live with us, they still need our influence.

Communicate Using Family Meetings

Family meetings are different than the weekly staff meetings. They involve everyone in the family. These are an ideal way to communicate changes in routines or to introduce new ones, particularly if the routine applies to all of the children or the whole family. These might be for things like how to act in a restaurant, how to act during a visit to Grandma's house, and how to keep things tidy and orderly. I wouldn't use the family meeting to talk about private, personal routines, like age-appropriate hygiene and so forth. You don't want to risk embarrassing your child in front of the other kids. In those cases, take them aside in the privacy of their room to talk and explain. Work with them one-on-one.

Present a Unified Front—Always

Mother and father must present a unified relationship at all times. This is paramount to a healthy, peaceful home. When mom and dad are united, it signals to the children that the marriage is secure and their parents are on the same page, especially in the training and discipline areas. Vow to each other to never disagree in front of the children. Agree to discuss disagreements in private, never in public. If a child realizes you are on different pages, they play one parent off the other one. Any chaos or arguing is leveraged as a diversion from their own actions and breaks the harmony and peace between the parents, which harms the respect levels within the family. This goes for divorced parents, too. Unity in raising your children together is huge.

If the other parent doesn't allow something that you would like to handle differently, suggest a private discussion on the matter. Don't debate in front of the children. Only in the case of significant physical or psychological damage should open disagreements between parents be allowed. If after discussing the issue in private you are not yet unified about something, then treat it as a situation in which no decision has been reached. You should tell the children that mom and dad are still discussing it. It is not a competition between who can win and who will lose. You are on the same team and the focus should be on working toward an agreement you can both live with.

Use Positive Reinforcement

Validate your children and praise them every time you notice something they did well. We covered this in the chapter on Respect, but it's worth talking about again here. When your child is doing positive things toward mastering one of the routines you're working on, or even one they've done for a while, stop and compliment them for it. Acknowledge that you notice them trying and can see them doing it and you're proud of them.

Parenting is really about installing good routines in your children and letting the routines become locked-in habits. Your children need lots of encouragement at the beginning of training to let them know that doing this is worth their while. They need rewards, appreciation, gratefulness, praise, trophies, and so forth. We all do this for getting them potty trained, and we need to do this for lots of other key routines they need to know.

Some routines will actually determine the success and/or failure of your children's lives, thing like:

> How to read and enjoy it.
>
> How to do basic arithmetic.
>
> How to brush their teeth.
>
> How to shower and clean themselves.
>
> An appropriate bedtime routine that lets them fall asleep and provides enough sleep every night.
>
> How to act appropriately at a meal.
>
> How to greet a stranger.
>
> How to act when they are frustrated.
>
> How to be quiet when they want to be noisy or active.
>
> How to dress themselves.
>
> How to pick up after themselves.

All of these and many other crucial routines are a few repetitive steps that can set them up for success. So praise them, appreciate them, reward them, cheer for them, make it a game with them. Your children will learn all of the above routines and many more if they get positive strokes while they are learning them. Remember that they want to please you. They want you to be proud of them. The more you find things that make you proud of them, the more they will want to get that reward again.

One father who was working with his boys on how to be kind to each other, stopped the whole family one night and yelled for the boys to come into the living room after they had just made their way into their rooms. He pointed out to everyone that the two brothers had done an excellent job of going down the hallway without punching, yelling, or saying anything mean to each other. The dad made it a big deal and praised them for it, rather than pointing out how they messed up on too many occasions.

Another father sat down and rewarded his son and daughter for getting parts of the multiplication table right with M&M's. While I don't know if rewarding children with candy is the best in every situation, it did motivate the children to try harder, and with that motivation, they were able to master the multiplication table that is theirs forever.

Dana and I had the problem of getting the girls to put their napkins on their laps before we started eating. So, we made it a game. If someone didn't have their napkin on their lap before we started eating, that person would have to stand up and sing a silly song. They loved the fact that one night I forgot, and I was the one who had to stand up and sing a silly song.

Many times, I made my children practice doing a routine right five times if I saw them doing it improperly. Then I would praise them for doing it right the last few times of the practice session. I wanted them to know how great the praise and appreciation felt that came from doing it right.

Get Help When You Need It!

We don't need to be stressed out about teaching the various routines, and we don't have to know everything. We just need to do the best we can at teaching positive and helpful routines to our children. If we discover that we don't know a positive or helpful routine for a given situation (like applying to college or swimming the butterfly stroke correctly), we can figure out who to ask to teach us or our children that routine or hire someone who does know. In fact, there are lots of things we don't know, which is why we have teachers, coaches, tutors, mentors, pastors, youth pastors, grandparents, big brothers and big sisters, and many others. Some people have special knowledge that we don't. That's okay! I can't tell you how many math tutors we used to try to get across various math problems that neither I nor my wife could explain.

If you need help, here are rhree practical things you can do:

1. Ask people you know who have raised successful children what they did specifically in the areas where you need help.
2. Read parenting books that detail these parts of raising kids.
3. Ask people you know if you can watch them go through these rituals and times with their kids.

Teaching Various Kinds of Routines

Recently, I have become more and more aware of how many of the crucial routines for parents are disappearing, and with them the ability to raise children to be functioning, independent adults. As a pastor I see it everywhere. There seem to be no consistent ways children are taught to get up in the morning. No consistent eating time or instructive activities are taking place during the eating time. There is no consistent way to go to bed. Fewer consistent habits are being communicated about personal hygiene. It is incumbent upon parents to instruct kids in the crucial routines for a successful life.

I think this is because either the parents don't know the key routines, or they just don't slow down long enough to think things through. How can they pass on what they do not know? How can they know what their kids need if they don't take regular time to examine what is lacking or see the warning signs that something is missing? In Deuteronomy 6:5–7, God instructs parents to drill the truths of the Ten Commandments into their children through regular rituals:

> "YOU SHALL LOVE THE LORD YOUR GOD WITH ALL YOUR HEART AND WITH ALL YOUR SOUL AND WITH ALL YOUR MIGHT.
>
> THESE WORDS, WHICH I AM COMMANDING YOU TODAY, SHALL BE ON YOUR HEART. YOU SHALL TEACH THEM *DILIGENTLY* TO YOUR SONS AND SHALL TALK OF THEM WHEN YOU SIT IN YOUR HOUSE AND WHEN YOU WALK BY THE WAY AND WHEN YOU LIE DOWN AND WHEN YOU RISE UP." (EMPHASIS MINE)

Teaching our kids is a full-time job. If we do not teach our children proper and helpful routines, they still need to learn them later in life, but it will be more difficult to absorb them, or they won't do them at all. Much of the military training is learning various routines that will assist a person in life—cleanliness routines, neatness routines, respect routines, hard-work routines, submission routines, physical health routines, follow-through routines, and so forth. Kids shouldn't need the military to teach them these things. They should learn them in the home.

As a child grows, many routines need to be taught and retaught over and over again. Please realize that just because you tell them or show them once, they will not know how to do it "right" from then on. You will need to explain, re-explain, and practice these things a number of times in the future. This is the joy of parenting. Don't get mad at your kids…instead, become a better coach and enjoy the process.

Moral Routines

For centuries, parents have adopted routines to communicate morality to their children. Parents had their children recite the Ten Commandments each evening at dinner so they could learn the basic ethical and moral lines of a civilized society. In Proverbs 4:1–5, Solomon tells of this routine of when his father, King David, taught him the Ten Commandments when he was a boy.

> HEAR, O SONS, THE INSTRUCTION OF A FATHER,
> AND GIVE ATTENTION THAT YOU MAY GAIN UNDERSTANDING,
>
> FOR I GIVE YOU SOUND TEACHING;
> DO NOT ABANDON MY INSTRUCTION.
>
> WHEN I WAS A SON TO MY FATHER, TENDER AND THE ONLY SON IN THE SIGHT OF MY MOTHER,
>
> THEN HE TAUGHT ME AND SAID TO ME,
> "LET YOUR HEART HOLD FAST MY WORDS;
> KEEP MY COMMANDMENTS AND LIVE;

Acquire wisdom! Acquire understanding!

Do not forget nor turn away from the words of my mouth.

In Jewish homes, it was the duty of fathers to spend time before dinner instructing the children in the Ten Commandments in such a way that the children understood these were the father's commands to the children. The wife was allowed to withhold dinner until this ritual was performed. When Solomon says "do not forget my commandments," he is asking the child to remember when the father instructed them in the Ten Commandments. It wasn't just God's laws; it was the father's instruction to the children. If you lived within these lines and acquired wisdom from them about how to live positively, then you would have a great life. This routine of learning from the father every night before dinner was an extremely valuable routine that helped generations to understand morality, ethics, and the principles of a great life.

My wife and I adopted this same routine into our family meal. We desperately wanted our girls to know where the ethical and moral lines were. What we found to be helpful was using placemats printed with the Ten Commandments on them to go under each of their plates (appendix 2). When the kids were small, before they could read, we all read the Ten Commandments together. The kids followed along as best they could. Soon they had them memorized.

Sometimes we would all say them and sometimes we quizzed them. They loved this game. And because they were so small, they had cute phrases for some of them, like "no altry" for "adultery," or in the case of no stealing, "no taking your sister's stuff and putting it in your underwear." That one would get a few laughs. Believe it or not, the teachings have stayed with them as adults. They know the moral foundations for life's decisions because of a routine we had at dinner when they were small.

We also made it clear that we are not saved by keeping the Ten Commandments because we cannot possibly keep them. We are only saved by the life, death, and resurrection of Jesus Christ. Children need to know the Ten Commandments. All children need a routine like this one.

Family Devotions

In addition to the Ten Commandments, we would talk about other passages, like the Lord's Prayer, the Beatitudes, the Fruit of the Spirit, the Apostles' Creed, and others. We used the evening meal to learn them and discuss how they related to their day (see appendix 2 for additional placemat ideas). We also talked about things I had read in the paper that day and what conclusions could be drawn from people's obedience to morality or disobedience to it. I was always on the lookout for moral lessons I could teach my girls. Talking about spiritual things was just a regular routine that we did at the beginning of dinner. It sometimes only lasted five minutes and many times sparked discussions that went all through dinner.

Sunday Routines

Sundays need their own routines too. What is different on Sunday? When does the family go to church? What are the systems around that process? Going to church is losing its status as a ritual and yet it is so important. It teaches that even parents have a boss, that learning keeps going no matter how old you are. It teaches relationships of an inter-generational nature are important. It teaches that God is important and first in our lives. It provides a chance to reinforce the biblical worldview.

Relational Routines

Kids need to be taught how to relate to other people and how to act in social situations. These lessons are not intuitive. Let's look at a few that are particularly helpful.

Eating Out Routines

What do the children do when the family goes out to eat? When Dana and I were trying to help our girls prepare to go out, we would have them practice eating slower and work with them to be able to sit still for an hour. We trained them to use the right fork and put the napkin in their lap. We practiced using quieter voices and keeping their hands to themselves, how to order, and what items would fit into our budget.

Elders Routines

What are the routines around greeting other adults? We required our children to greet adults who came to the home with respect, so we required that they call them Mr. or Mrs. or Ms. Even the babysitter was Miss Linda or Miss Kate. It taught them to respect the authority of the person they were speaking to. Those terms and how to greet different people need to be taught to your children through the use of routines.

Different families have different terms of endearment for grandparents and close friends or relatives. Have your children practice greeting grandma before she gets there so that they are clear how to get it right before grandma is actually there. You don't want your child's first try at a routine to be in a pressure-packed situation.

I have for years trained young men in wedding parties how to usher people to their seats in just a few minutes. Say, "May I escort you to your seat." Offer them your arm. Walk slowly until you get to the right row. Extend your other arm to show them that this is where they should sit. These little routines set someone up to be successful at a particular aspect of life. There are hundreds of these that parents should teach their children.

We used to have practice sessions before we actually went into see grandma and grandpa. We would say, "Here is what is going to happen and here is what you should do." "Now, you practice that like I am grandma." Every greeting is usually a series of four to eight things that you do and then the other person does. Go over this information with your children and have them practice so that they can perform this greeting routine flawlessly.

Also teach them how to shake hands when they meet someone new or as a greeting for someone they already know. Handshaking is important to convey confidence. Children also need to know about how to treat elderly people, like giving up their seat or opening doors for them. Help them understand that older people have physical challenges and sometimes need a little extra help or time.

Store Routines

Before we would enter a store at the mall or wherever, I would go over again how they were to behave. I can't tell you how many times I explained to our girls outside a store that during this trip, we were going to put our hands behind our back and walk through the store calmly. We were not going to run or touch anything, but we would be commenting on all the different things that looked interesting to us. I would put my hands behind my back, then the girls would do the same, and finally mom would put her hands behind her back and we would enter the store. We would snake through the different isles and would have lively conversation about various items, but we (none of us) were touching anything.

We also had buying trips to stores and we would explain what that would look like outside the stores before we went in. We were going to purchase certain items. We would go to those sections of the store and look at the goods, then take them down from the shelf and decide whether we were going to actually purchase them or not. If we decided we would not purchase them, we would put them back. If we decided to buy them, then we would put them in the cart or walk them quietly and calmly to the cash register and purchase them. As the children got older, we would give them the money so they could have the experience of actually handling the money and interacting with the clerk.

Guest Routines

What happens when guests come over, either their own friends or your adult guests? There are certain things that children must be prepared to do differently when guests come into their house. Also, keep in mind some of their own routines won't change when their friends come over. Be sure to help your children understand which routines need to be added and which ones need to stay.

Day-to-Day Routines

These are the routines that teach kids how to get by successfully in life day-to-day.

Waking Up Routines

How can your children wake up well and what does that look like? What time should they wake up during the week versus the weekend? What should they do upon first waking up? We had our girls tell us three things they were thankful for and remember and repeat a Scripture they had read last night. What should a person do first when they get out of bed? Make the bed, use the rest room, shower and prepare for the day, sit and read quietly for a few minutes, go and greet their parents, put on their clothing for the day, and so forth. All of these are options to explore. Do they eat with the family at breakfast? What time is that meal served? Parents have the ability to help their children develop powerful habits that will help them all through their life.

Morning Routines

What do children do in the morning before they have to leave for school and/or dad goes off to work? This can be a good time for chores. This can be a time for finishing homework. This can be a time for helping with the siblings, even practicing an instrument. Parents get to decide what happens in this time and the children will see it as a ritual. I realize many families today start their day so early trying to get everyone to school on time—every family's routines will look differently.

Eating and Dinnertime Routines

Children do not know how to eat properly, so parents must teach them. We must teach them how to eat with silverware. We must teach them how to eat slowly and make the meal last. We must teach them how to let other people talk during a meal. We must teach them how to enter into other people's conversations and not change the subject to what we want to talk about. We must teach them the value of getting together each day and sharing. Meal times are perfect for reconnecting with family and friends at school. Teach your children how to use that time wisely.

Also, it's good to step back every once-in-a-while to reevaluate the way you do things. For example, one thing my wife wishes she would have done differently was how she handled snacks. She didn't really regulate or plan for snacks, and things might have worked more smoothly at our house if she'd done some things differently. I still think she did a great job, though.

During dinner, we can also give a spiritual lesson and establish the value of God in our life through prayer and discussions about various issues in the wider world. Sadly, one of the most destructive things I have recently seen is to have all sports practices are being scheduled during dinner time so that the family never gets to have meals together. Fight against this and find a way to have a meal together before or after practice, or don't participate in that sport or that league.

Evening Routines

Evenings in the typical house is different than during the day. It is a time of homework, games, fun, talking, projects, chores, and love. How will that be done in your house? Today, it is too easy to fall into a time of watching TV and everyone going their own way on various devices. There are other things to do that are way more valuable. Yes, they take effort, but they are so worth it. What is the order of homework and fun? Some families have dinner, then a little fun, and then homework. Some families work on homework, then have dinner, then have a little fun. This time is up for grabs and the parents get to build a system into the child about what to do to make the family close and to ensure each person in the family is ready for the next day.

Bedtime Routines

A child needs a routine for going to bed. In fact, all of us need a routine. We cannot just stop doing one activity, lie down, and fall asleep. Children need to realize by doing the routine that they need to start getting ready for bed about an hour before they want to be asleep. They need to have a consistent and clean place where they will sleep. They need to clean up their room before they go to sleep. They need to get into their bed clothing. Some families shower and bathe at night. They need to brush and floss their teeth. They need to gather with their parents for a recap of the day with a focus on what was positive. They need to pray and be prayed over. They need to be given something to think about as they fall asleep, like a story or words of love and encouragement and/or Scripture.

One of Dana's favorite things to do when our girls were young was to read to them at bedtime. She and the girls usually took a trip to the library once a week and had a ton of books to read. She loved making the stories more fun and creative by embellishing some of the stories, adding voices, and the like. This is such a great way to bond with your kids, and they love it. Kids thrive with story time.

This ritual will change somewhat when the children reach the teen years as they need more independence from their parent's participation in their bedtime rituals. I would suggest that you not let them listen to music that is rebellious, hate-filled, or loud as your children go to bed. I'm a firm believer that doing so puts these messages into their subconscious and they live them out the next day. During the teen years, your children need to talk to you. Wise parents will be ready to really listen at the times when the teens want to talk. I found those to be late at night between 11:00 p.m. and 1:00 a.m. It was during those times when I learned the most about what my kids were going through and when I helped them the most.

Personal Hygiene Routines

These rituals include how one cares for their teeth, such as brushing, flossing, using mouthwash; how one uses the restroom (wiping oneself, flushing the toilet); and bathing/showering (how often, cleansing all parts of the body, soap, drying off, hanging the towel). As girls get older, they need to know how to take care of their hair, how to be safe with makeup, body hair, menstruation hygiene, and pierced ears. Boys need to know how to take care of facial hair and body odor.

Family Routines

Family routines teach the children how to have the best relationship and time with the members of their own family. What are the routines that the family does together throughout the week or on an outing or vacation to make time as a family special?

Midweek Routines

Usually in the middle of the week, families do something different. It is up to the parents what they want it to be. Do you play a particular game on Tuesday? Do you go to church on Wednesday? Do you as a family all watch a program together on Thursday? It may be a certain game or ritual with the parents. It could be going out to a particular restaurant before church on Wednesday night. Children and parents need something to look forward to during the middle of the week so life doesn't get too monotonous.

I can remember taking each of my daughters on a date during the middle of the week. We went and did something together just the two of us. Many times, it didn't involve spending much money, but it was time for me and one of my girls to spend an hour together that week. This was a great time.

Vacation and/or Holiday Routines

One of the most interesting changes to routines is vacations and/or holidays. There is often a lot of anger that bubbles out in the midst of vacations and holidays because there are all of these clashing expectations. "I thought we would be doing this." "Well, I thought we would be doing this other thing." "I want to do this if it is going to be a vacation." "I don't relax when we are doing that."

Every parent has the ideal vacation or holiday in their mind. What they will be doing. When it starts. What the children will be doing. How many activities each day. Do we sleep in or get an early start? In our family, we like to do at least three things each day to enjoy vacation days: one in the morning, one in the afternoon, and one in the evening. So, we needed to get our kids up-to-speed on this routine. We did find that at times we crammed too much in a day for the children when they were small, and they may have slept through the second and/or third activity. We adjusted when necessary.

Realize that if everybody knows what the vacation or holiday routine is, there is less anger. There can be practice on how to act at the Thanksgiving meal or opening gifts at Christmas. You as the parents get to set the routines. It doesn't have to be the same ones you had when you were growing up; it can be something totally new. It's up to you.

Conclusion

Looking at this list of routines, I know you could feel overwhelmed. But realize that you already have opinions on what good routines in each of these areas are like and maybe you're already doing them. Both you and your spouse have ideas about this. Talk together, work through the various ideas, get counsel from others, and inject them into your children's lives. Times for these routines will happen whether you plan them or not. This is why the staff meeting is so important every week. One parent or the other will suggest that a particular routine is needed to be taught or retaught. This is what should happen. Add new routines and you will watch your children adapt and build successful routines into their lives. Use these times to talk with your children about how encouraged you are with them. Notice the things they have done and are doing. Ask them to tell you about what they want to do.

I cannot possibly tell you all the routines that will help launch your children to a wonderful life, and each family will handle aspects of life differently. But that is the wonder and joy of family. Your children need routines and they need to know how to handle all of these different things; this will bring your approval and will allow them to succeed in the outside world.

As I said before, you will often not know that a routine is missing until something goes wrong in the family. Them not doing it properly, if at all, is a sign that they do not really have the routine down. It takes patience and wisdom, sometimes weeks and months, to teach and practice a new routine until it becomes second nature, but doing so will pay dividends for years to come.

Questions to Ask at the Weekly Staff Meeting:

- What routines do the kids just not know to do correctly?
- What irritates you the most about the kids and their routines this week?
- What three-to-ten-step routine would fix that problem?
- Is a particular routine the most important thing for our sanity or our family this week?
- What routines are the kids getting right that they used to have a problem with? How can we praise them for this?
- Are there any routines that we cannot teach well and we should delegate to someone else?

6.
responsibility

If you've never seen the movie *The Miracle Worker*, you should. This is the movie of how Helen Keller was raised and trained by Anne Sullivan to "hear," "speak," and learn. Helen Keller was born blind and deaf, and considered by most to be a wild child incapable of normal life or civilized interaction. Her parents hired Anne Sullivan to try and reach their child. Anne Sullivan spelled with her fingers into the hands of Helen the names for things *thousands of times*. Helen had no idea what these finger movements in her palm meant. But then one day, Helen felt the water from the pump as Ann spelled water for the thousandth time in her hand and then Helen spelled the word "water" back to Anne Sullivan. Anne Sullivan shouted, "She knows!" It was an overwhelming emotional moment as Helen began to understand how to communicate with the outside world. This movie is one of the best motion pictures for training our children how to be responsible—the true story of how one little girl, who was locked in a body that didn't see or hear, came to learn and communicate and act in a civilized manner.[6]

As the parent, you are similarly working to help your children understand the world around them and the rules that govern this foreign environment. You will have to explain thousands of times what is expected and how to behave, and only after what seems way too long will they understand. We have eighteen to twenty-one years to teach all the customs, skills, language, patterns, and routines our children will need to live in the adult world. Be patient, persistent, and clear because they really don't understand without you teaching them. One time explaining will not be enough. They are little, their bodies are growing, their minds are processing all kinds of information, feelings, actions, and reactions. Someday they will amaze you with all they are capable of if you will realize they are blind and deaf to all the rules, ideas, customs, and traditions you know. Keep at this important work; one day your children will astound you with all they can do, know, produce, and express.

Six Things We Are All Responsible For

God says clearly in the scriptures that all of us are responsible for six things that shape the whole of our life. This includes our children. What are they?

Everything we choose.
(Galatians 6:7)

Everything we think.
(2 Corinthians 10:3–5; Philippians 4:7,8)

Everything we say.
(Proverbs 18:21; Ephesians 4:29)

Everything we do.
(Romans 2:6)

Everything we emote.
(Philippians 2:3–10)

Every motive we have.
(Proverbs 16:2)

That's a lot to be responsible for! That's why responsibility is a crucial lesson we must help teach. Being responsible means, "I take responsibility for my body, my words, my emotions, my actions, and my attitudes." The choices we make create the life we live, which is the basic law of reaping and sowing (Gal. 6:7). People from all different kinds of backgrounds, advantages, and disadvantages have great lives. Great lives come from great choices. Yes, there is evil and oppression in our world, but it is the choices we make that define us. We must teach our children that *they* are responsible for their choices. We cannot control everything about our world, but we can control our choices, and our choices will create our world. Even children who were born in poverty or oppressed situations can begin to make good choices and create a different path than others in their same circumstances.

The best type of child is not the perfect child but the responsible child. Does your child take responsibility for their choices about what they choose to say; for what they choose to do; for what they choose to think; for why they choose to do something; for the attitude and emotions they choose to have? All children will make mistakes and act immaturely. This is the growing-up process. They will need our correction to help them see what they did wrong or didn't do at all and replace it with the responsible choice. Here are some examples of what correction could look like:

> *Now, young man, you made a choice there and it caused chaos. What choice could you have made that would have resulted in a different reaction by everyone?*

> *Young lady, you made a choice to slam the door when you went in your room. You disrespected me and you disrespected my property. Let's have you come out and make a different choice with the door.*

> *I notice that you made a choice not to clean your room, so I am going to have to help you be motivated to clean your room. I could take away your Xbox privileges until it is clean. I could stand here and tell you exactly what to do and watch you do it. I could throw away anything that is on the floor when I come back in fifteen minutes. I could have you clean this little section in the next fifteen minutes and then come back every fifteen minutes as you clean various sections in this room. Which way do you want me to help you?*

By teaching them responsibility, you are trying to teach them to discern how their actions have different reactions in other people: some good, some bad, some disastrous, and some powerfully delightful. They are learning and growing how to live in the world they have been placed in. It is our joy as parents to help them grow up and learn wise choices from foolish ones they make. It is a sacred trust and a delight to see your children get wiser as they learn from you to discern from the choices presented to them. The key message you are trying to communicate to your children is this truth:

I am accountable for all my choices.

The Bible talks about this responsibility training in various places in the scriptures.

> "Correct your son, and he will give you comfort; He will also delight your soul. Where there is no vision, the people are unrestrained, But happy is he who keeps the law. A slave will not be instructed by words alone; For though he understands, there will be no response."
>
> —Proverbs 29:17–19

This whole section in the book of Proverbs talks about how children must know what is expected. They must be corrected back to that standard. They must be shown, not just told.

> "FOOLISHNESS IS BOUND UP IN THE HEART OF A CHILD; THE ROD OF DISCIPLINE WILL REMOVE IT FAR FROM HIM."
>
> —PROVERBS 22:15

Here we learn about children's natural self-focus. All children start out completely self-focused. It is their natural starting place. When the Bible talks about foolishness, this refers to a person's natural orientation toward self-focus and selfishness. They must overcome this tendency to only care about themselves and what they want, and they need to take into account the other people in their life and how their actions and inactions affect their world.

One of my children responded to a family question we asked, "What are you thinking about?" with the comment, "I am thinking about myself." This was so honest and true. We got her a little sweatshirt with the saying on it, "It is time to start thinking about Me." It is the parents' job to lovingly guide the children into an appreciation of the wider world and how they fit into it.

When we hand a young adult to the world at ages eighteen to twenty-one, we need them to know what exactly they are responsible for and to feel the consequences (good and bad) from their actions. We can teach them while they are at home that how they close a door is a choice; how they roll their eyes is a choice; how they dress is a choice; their attitude is a choice; what they say is a choice. Too often in our society we go on autopilot and just parrot back what is around us and then wonder why others are upset with us. Children need to clearly understand that certain kinds of actions, words, and attitudes get positive reactions from their parents and others, while other kinds of actions, words, and attitudes get negative reactions from their parents and others.

Children and teens have no idea what they are facing in the world. They do not understand they are headed into a dog-eat-dog world that is largely unforgiving. It is a world of cause and effect. Everything they do, say, and emote brings about an effect. They don't cause everything, but God has placed them in a cause-and-effect world. They can change their world by the choices they make. If they want a good life, then they must increasingly evaluate the impact their choices will bring about before they make them.

Here are a few examples:

- If I scream at my sister, how will she and the rest of the family react?
- If I pitch a fit here in the store, will I get what I want and what will happen after?
- If I punch my brother, will he tell on me and get me in trouble?
- If I study hard for this test, will I get a better grade and what do I get for that?
- If I greet mom and dad's friends graciously, then I stand a better chance to get a job this summer.
- If I ask dad "How much longer before we get there?" one more time, will he get mad and stay mad the rest of way to the amusement park?

Getting kids to take responsibility for the things that they choose will give them the key to move their life forward and not become a victim of other people's choices. All of the techniques and ideas in this chapter are designed to teach your children to make a better choice the next time they are confronted with a situation. You have eighteen to twenty-one years to help them realize that they are responsible for everything they choose. If they choose to work hard and get good grades, then they are responsible for that. If they start smoking dope or drinking alcohol, they are making that choice and will bear the responsibility for the results. This element of the Six R's of a joy-filled family is monumental.

What Are Children Responsible For?

Let's take a look at some areas of responsibility for the various age levels.

Pre-School Age

When children are small, they have only a few areas of needed responsibility. It was a great comfort to me to see that the list was small when the children were small. When you are training them, remember your children do not know anything. They don't know how to please you, and they do not know what to do after only one explanation, so keep teaching, practicing, and re-teaching.

Pre-School Age Responsibilities

Sleep: going to sleep, staying asleep, crises, naps, waking up from sleep
Eating: getting ready, sitting still, being done, cleaning up
Playing: getting started, toys, ending, cleaning up
Bathroom needs: alert, process, time, clean up, check back
Getting attention: how to get it and how to wait
Staying: standing, sitting, quiet, movement
Exploring/touching: permission, safety, climbing
Adults: greeting, approval, danger
Cleaning up: everything has to be cleaned up

Say things like, "This is *what* we do…" and "This is *how* we do…" in every one of the above areas. If they don't learn the basic routines, then trouble compounds from there. Yes, you will have to train and retrain hundreds of times about how to go to sleep; how to eat properly; how to go to the bathroom; how to stay in place; how to get your attention; how to clean up after playing, but eventually they will get it. These are building blocks to start from.

I read a story about a famous research scientist who had made several significant medical breakthroughs. He was asked why he was able to achieve more than the average person—what set him so far apart from others? Remarkably, he attributed it to a lesson his mother had taught him when he was only two years old. He was trying to carry a bottle of milk out of the fridge and lost his grip, of course he spilled the milk all over the floor. Instead of his mother getting angry, she used it as a learning opportunity. She said, "What a wonderful mess you've made! I've rarely seen such a huge puddle of milk. Well, the damage is already done. Would you like to get down and play in the milk before we clean it up?"

Of course, he did so, being a two-year-old little boy after all, and a few minutes later, his mother said, "You know, whenever you make a mess like this, eventually you have to clean it up. So how would you like to do that? We could use a towel, sponge, or mop. Which do you prefer?" After they finished cleaning up the milk, she said, "What we have here is a failed experiment in how to carry a big bottle of milk with two tiny hands. Let's go out in the backyard, fill the bottle with water, and see if you can discover a way to carry it without dropping it." And they did.

The scientist learned that day that mistakes happen and he didn't have to be afraid to make them. They were just opportunities to learn something new, which is what science is all about.[7] This is just the kind of thinking we need to have with our children, turning a mistake or a mess into a learning opportunity, while exercising patience and intentionality.

Elementary-School Age

In the elementary years, the areas of responsibility grow. Again, let me say that you will need to explain over and over how to do these new responsibilities that will come at your children as they go to school and encounter new friends. Some of your children will not listen to what you are telling them at first and they will try it their way, which will create some difficulties. This is good because you can let them get the lessons from the consequences and then come back and say, "Here is how we handle this area of choices in our life." Over and over you will be training them how to be successful in that routine and area of their life. At some point if you are persistent and clear, it will click just like it did with Helen Keller, and they will adopt your methods.

Elementary School Age Responsibilities

School: getting ready for school, being at school, interacting with the teacher, coming home from school;

Homework: when to start on homework, levels of effort on homework;

Friends: how to make friends, how to keep friends, signs of a bad friend, levels of friendship;

Feelings: what feelings are, what they are for, when to pay attention to them, when to ignore them;

Status: what is status, why do some have it and others do not, watching out for the little guy, watching out for the bully;

Siblings: how to treat your siblings, how to protect yourself from your siblings, how to love your siblings;

Attitudes: what are attitudes, what do attitudes do, choosing a different attitude, people's reactions to attitudes, trying on different attitudes;

Media: how much media is too much, what is media doing to me, the distraction level of media, the truth or lies of media.

Teen Years

In the teen years, responsibility grows even more as teens enter into the realm of driving, dating, jobs, social freedoms, spending money, and the like. New routines now must be taught. Your children are only a few years away from being adults where the world will not care about them the way you do and will not forgive them for irresponsibility.

Teenage Years Responsibilities

Driving: learning to drive, insurance, maintaining the car, gassing the car, fixing the car;

Romance: feelings for someone, the power of feelings, breaking up, how far touching can go, how to talk to a romantic friend;

Increasing independence: choices when the parents aren't there, choices different than your parents, what are your passions and interests?

Finances: earning, managing, saving and giving money, financial literacy;

Future: what do you want the future to look like, how will you get there, who will you get to help you, filling up the nine relational gardens with love;

Parental relationships: transitioning to an adult relationship with parents, allowing them to help you, allowing them to guide you;

Fun: what types of fun are you drawn to, what types of damaging fun are you drawn to, what types of people are in each type of fun?

Media: how will you regulate your social media, what will you stay away from, how is media lying to you, how is media tell you the truth?

Realize that every time your children messes up a choice, it is a chance to teach the right routine again, the right choice, the right method instead of the one they choose. The foundation that you have taught them of making a responsible choice in the elementary years will help them navigate the new opportunities and temptations that come with the teen years. The first ten years of parenting are years of direct teaching, and the second eight are much more Socratic. Ask them things like, "What do you think will happen if you were to go ahead and do that idea?" "Who have you known who has done that?"

A number of wise parents sometimes have one child or even one parent go rogue and get into drugs or affairs or criminal activity. This is such a tough issue for everybody involved. One kid came out great, but one kid or parent made really bad choices. What do you do in those cases? I do not condemn parents when one of their children rebels or gets sucked into a life of addiction. It usually suggests that one of the Six R's was missing during some portion or all of the upbringing of that family. This is why I often refer to the Six R's as the ingredients in great families. When one of the R's is left out of raising our children, it can have disastrous results in the family and individual children.

Many times, a child who goes rogue is expressing their individuality and need for independence and they will come to understand the wisdom of much of what their parents did to raise them. It can also suggest that the person who went rogue responded to the temptations or pressures around them in a poor way. They missed a key understanding of their responsibility—*every choice you make is your responsibility.*

But the good news is that the forgiveness of God is everlasting, and many times the wayward one is able to come back to a great life and loving relationships through confession, forgiveness, and repentance. We hear all the time of prodigal children who come back to the faith and fold of the family. This allows the family to rally around this person and embrace them and, in many cases, surround them with the Six R's again.

Yes, good kids can make really bad choices that will change their lives forever. That is a key truth in responsibility—*everyone is responsible for their choices.* Any hole you are standing in, you dug or helped to dig. You can climb out. You will need help. It will be hard, but there are all kinds of people who are there to help you, and most importantly, God is not condemning you. He wants everyone to have a great life more than they do. A great family is built around the cooperation of all the individuals participating in the Six R's thereby creating a lasting and deeply enjoyable bond.

Teaching Your Children Responsibility

Teaching children responsibility takes creativity, ingenuity, and patience. Each family is different but the goal is a child who makes a better choice the next time. One family will rely on time outs, and one will rely on practice. A third family will use rewards, and a fourth family is going to explain everything to the children and use logic.

The Six R's of Wise Parenting: Responsibility

Training your children to become responsible citizens and God-honoring people requires both positive and negative methods. These surprisingly boil down to just a few basic ways. The scriptures consistently talk about two broad ways to teach your children to be responsible for their actions: "The Rod" and "Reproof." It is best to understand these two ways as parents "taking action" and/or "using words." There are some children and some situations where responsibility is taught and embraced through words. There are other times when some children and some situations require parental action or child action. Through these two methods, we train our children to become increasingly responsible for their behaviors, words, attitudes, and emotions.

Note: Every training and discipline technique must be designed to cause better choices next time, or it is useless.

If you have a very compliant child, then you may only need to use mild words to change their behavior to conform with what you are directing them. But if you have a strong-willed child, then you will work much more heavily on

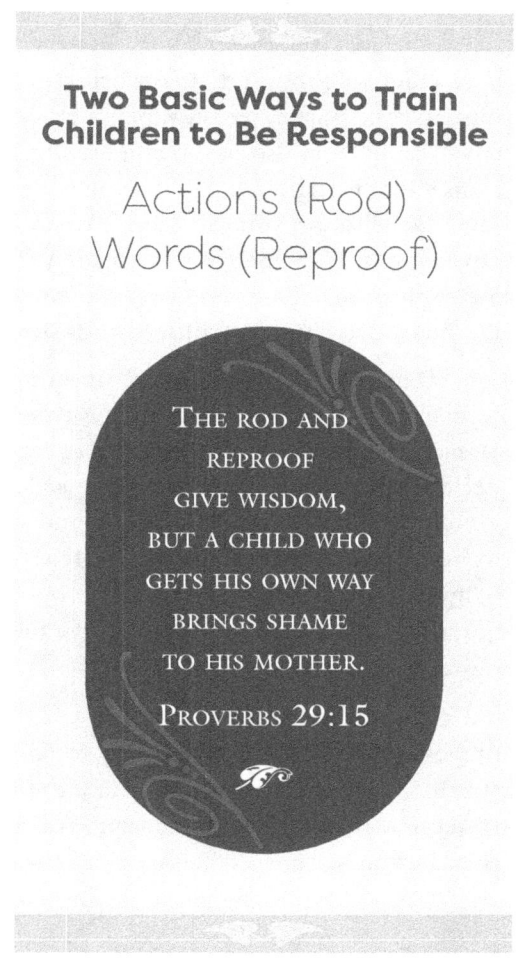

Two Basic Ways to Train Children to Be Responsible

Actions (Rod)
Words (Reproof)

THE ROD AND REPROOF GIVE WISDOM, BUT A CHILD WHO GETS HIS OWN WAY BRINGS SHAME TO HIS MOTHER.

PROVERBS 29:15

the actions side of the training for children who often resist you in everything. They really do want you to parent them, but they have a stronger, built-in resistance to direction, especially once they have gone through puberty. Love them and direct them because they need it.

The goal is responsibility not punishment. We see these two methods in how God deals with us and how various biblical parents succeeded and failed to teach their children responsibility. The issue is not how they messed up, but how will they act the next time they are in that situation? They will make mistakes, sometimes because of ignorance; sometimes because of lack of experience or rebellion. Whatever the reason for the misbehavior, the goal is always the same: *the child will learn responsibility for their actions, their words, their bodies, their attitudes, their emotions.*

The goal is not your comfort or the release of your anger. The goal is that your child will be responsible when they leave your home. It is usually best if husband and wife agree on which methods will be used for which offenses for which child. It is also best if you preplan how you will deal with certain situations and misdeeds. It is okay if you handled it a certain way the first time you saw this behavior; you can change to another more appropriate technique the next time. It is the parent's prerogative to change the training techniques. Be aware there may be times when you will need to use techniques and training methods that are new or different for you.

Dana and I used the weekly meeting to discuss and decide the best ways to help the kids make a better choice the next time. Sometimes we had a difference of opinion and we talked our way through the various positions and decided on a course of action. We needed to agree on which issues we were going after in each of the children and which methods we were planning on using. We would make signs for the refrigerator, the bathroom mirror, and the hallway to remind us which issues we were focusing on and which ones we were ignoring, along with the agreed-upon method for training responsibility into our girls.

I have a list at the end of this chapter discussing all of the various techniques to help teach responsibility to your children. It can be helpful to post this list on the refrigerator so you are not without a cheat sheet when something new comes up. Remember to stay calm; you and they will get through this latest immaturity. They are just growing up and mistakes are natural.

Correction Techniques

In this section I have listed a number of ways to apply these two broad correction categories—words (reproof) and actions (rod) to train children to become responsible. You will most likely invent some new ways that really fit your personality and parenting style. If you prefer a particular training methodology but it is not working (i.e., the child is not changing their behavior), then don't hesitate to change to another technique.

Words Techniques (Reproof)

Here are some basic ways of using *words* to teach our children to be responsible. We all hope that these will be enough to persuade our children to change their words, actions, and thinking, but they are not always enough. It is good to start here.

Set Clear Expectations

Be clear about what is acceptable behavior in a situation or circumstance. A child cannot be expected to read minds. They really don't know how to behave at dinner unless you train them. Without your training, they really don't know how to act at grandma's house or how to ride in the car. They really don't know what to do with the impulse to move, cry, punch their sibling, and so on, until you train them. They really don't know how to get up, make the bed, put their pajamas away, shower, and head down to breakfast in thirty minutes, or how to clean themselves after they use the restroom.

This is the first discipline procedure, the first training method, the first action for developing an enjoyable family full of responsible individuals. For Dana and I, every time we were about to enter a different environment or setting, we had a sixty-second training meeting that told them what we expected them to do. We didn't talk about what we didn't want them to do. Instead, we used it as a positive training meeting: "Here is what we are going to do." For example:

> *You are going to sit down and listen to grandma tell her stories. If you need to go the rest room, you will get off your chair and come over to me and put your hand on my shoulder until I turn to you and ask "What do you want?" Only one of you can go to the bathroom at a time.*

Restate Expectations

Sometimes it is sufficient to restate the expectations and have the child re-say them. This practice alone produces the sufficient amount of learning needed so that the negative behavior will not reoccur. This entails potentially asking the child what they were supposed to do in that situation rather than what they did do. Making the child restate the expectations three times or restating them yourself to the child three times may be sufficient for the proper correction of behavior.

Verbal Repetition ("Tell me what I expect.")

This is where a parent will ask the child to tell them what the parent is expecting in detail. The children need to be able to tell the parents what they could or should have done. If they cannot do this quickly, then this is an opportunity for retraining. It is not a time to get upset at the children; it is just like Helen Keller's training. What is really wanted has not sunk in yet. Retrain them again without anger or resentment. They need to see and hear it again.

Ask them to tell you how you expect them to behave for the next thirty minutes. Say, "We are about to eat at a restaurant; what do I expect you to do in there for the next thirty minutes?" If they cannot tell you, then they don't know. If they can tell you what they need to do to please you, then congratulate them immensely for knowing the answer. Also praise them profusely when they do it.

Some children will love this type of question and others will not. If you start doing this when they are small and make a game of it, then it will be a wonderful way to help your children think ahead. It is like a pop-quiz in school. You want them to get the answers right. You want to be praising them and encouraging them for how smart they are to remember how to behave in all of these different situations and environments. It will also give you another reason to praise your children before they even start behaving correctly. They don't have to get the answer perfect to receive praise, especially at first, but they do need to get a few of the right answers with you helping them fill in the rest.

I always find parents amazed that their children do not know what you are expecting them to be like. You may have told them fifteen times before but they can't remember or are hoping that it will be different this time. But you just never know if the child may have had a trauma in their life today that caused them to forget what is expected of them. Their best friend may not have wanted to play with them. The dog barked at them. They couldn't play with their favorite toy for some reason. Your children (especially small children) need to be treated positively and helpfully. Help them pass the test they are about to take. They are about to get ready for bed; here are the answers to the test.

Verbal Reminder

Some children are so sensitive and in an emotional or chronological place where just a simple reminder of what they should have done is all they can handle. If a simple verbal rebuke or look of disappointment over what they did will cause them to not do the behavior again, there is no need to do anything more.

Praise (Verbal, Written, Tangible)

So much progress can be made in a child's life with praise. A child can be powerfully moved to responsible behavior over time through verbal, written, and/or tangible praise. Tell the child what they are doing right, even if it is only a small portion of the whole. Write a note to the child that you believe in them and areas where you see them succeeding. Give the child a ribbon, a trophy, a gift that symbolizes progress toward the goal or completion of the goal. Everyone wants to know that they are doing a good job. Sometimes we can be such perfectionists that we withhold praise until the child does it perfectly; that time never comes because they lost motivation while they were trying to get there.

Wise parenting takes patience, but it is a positive process of getting your child ready for the adult world. Don't let parenting become a negative process of constantly correcting your children. Parenting should be a loving process of encouraging, directing, gently correcting, and being loved by your child. Bathe your parenting process in love and encouragement and a joyful family will emerge. Major on the positives not the negatives.

Verbal Praise Tips

Say things like, "You did really great on this part; I'm proud of you!"

Don't hold out for perfection to praise them.

Give immediate positive feedback for everything they did right.

The more you are pleased with them, the more they will want to please you.

Written Praise Tips

Write a note, send a text, put it in their backpack or lunch box. "You did really great on this part; I'm proud of you."

Written notes telling them what they did right can mean a lot to them.

They can look back on them when they are most able to receive praise.

Do this weekly so they are swimming in praise; schedule praise so it comes regularly.

> ### Tangible Praise Tips
>
> Get a trophy; make a plaque; purchase a gift;
> give a weekly prize; provide a treat;
> reward them; play a game with them.
>
> You get to wear the special t-shirt this week.
> Here is a plaque with your name on it.
> Here is what Daddy is pleased with this week.
> Let's go get a prize.
>
> Tie the blessings to their actions and
> reactions from last week.
>
> A birthday gift can be a part of this process.

Intense Emotional Reminder

This is where normal discussions and words are not breaking through. The parent gets right down on the child's level so that you look into their eyes and let them know three things:

1. How you feel about what they did;
2. What they did that was wrong;
3. That you still love them but this must stop.

I have seen this type of verbal rebuke break through because it is emotional on several levels and absolutely clear.

Moral Reasoning: Ask the Five Questions

At times it is most helpful to have a moral reasoning conversation with your child about behavior that was wrong. When the child is in the elementary years and older, they can begin reasoning with you about their behaviors and the choices that led to them. Do not try this with a two-year-old. Some children are ready for this type of exchange at eight or nine and some a few years after this. In this conversation, you are going to ask them five questions and get answers from them. Most of this is adapted from Dr. William Glasser and his very helpful work with positive addiction.[8]

Q1: What did you do? *Not why, but what.*

Q2: Was that the right thing or the wrong thing to do in that situation?

Q3: What could you have done other than what you did?

Q4: What do we need to do so that you will never forget to make a different choice next time?

Q5: What will you choose next time?

Whatever was decided in the fourth question needs to be administered. This helps your child understand that they do have a choice and they do not need to just follow their impulses. (It is important to notes at times the outlandish training ideas that your children will come up with on step four. Keep in mind it needs to be training not torture.)

Earned Responsibility

This is where the parent and the child have set up an agreement that this child can gain this new level of responsibility if they act in a certain way in a certain situation. It is a verbal contract and can motivate some children to become responsible for their attitude, words, and actions.

Contract

In a number of instances of teenagers and their growing need for independence, it can be important to put in writing what they agree to do and what the parents agree to do. This is not for every situation, but it can be helpful in some situations where the child feels like they are not being heard or allowed to grow up. It should spell out the new abilities if they achieve the new level of responsibilities and the consequences if they do not.

Deal with the Guilt

Parents need to remember that children have true guilt when they have done something that they know is wrong. They need to be forgiven for what they did and told it will not affect the family dynamic or relationship as they go forward. They need to confess to what they have done and make plans to choose differently in the future. They need in many cases for the parent to say that they are forgiven.

Do not believe that they will just get over it and be okay. Help them work through what it means to restore the relationship and let them know that nothing they did or will do will eliminate them from being loved and in the family.

See appendix 4 for an overview of the Words (Reproof) consequence options. I have found it helpful to have this on the refrigerator so that you can have ideas of what to do in the spur of the moment when raising your kids.

Action Techniques (The Rod)

The following are the basic ways of using parental and child actions to train responsibility. These are sometimes the best and only ways to teach children (and adults) to take full responsibility for their actions, thoughts, words, and emotions. Many times, it is a combination of Words and Actions that will bring about responsibility. Remember you are not trying to make your children a clone of yourself or a robot doing what you do. You are trying to develop a young adult who will think, speak, and act in a responsible manner when they are on their own in a few years.

Demonstrate

This should almost always be the go-to technique because it will be needed much more than you think it should. This is where the parent demonstrates to the children the desired positive behavior. Focus on what is wanted not what is not wanted. Say, "Here is what I want you to do," then show them. Often it is important to have the children then be allowed or made to do it themselves. Scripture says, "A slave will not be instructed by words alone, for those he understands, there will be no response" (Prov. 29:19). This applies to children as well. When a child does not perform what is expected, then the child may need another demonstration. They may need to see you help them clean their room, explaining how it is to be done.

If the parent can demonstrate the desired behavior or have an older sibling demonstrate the upcoming behavior, it is a great visual model of what to do. I used to put my hands behind my back and hold them as I modeled how we would go through the stores so that we would not accidently touch things. All the girls would put their hands behind their back and we would walk through the stores commenting but not touching.

> *We're going to sit in the chair and read our books and color.*
>
> *We're going to speak when spoken to and look at grandma when she speaks to you (or whoever is speaking to us).*

Resist the urge to go over all the wrong ways of behaving. Don't put the emphasis on what not to do, or that is all they will get from this lesson. You may have to cover a couple of don't do's, but the emphasis should be on the right behaviors and the right actions. Let them try the right actions. Let them show you that they know how to do what you want.

Sometimes parents expect too much from their children, like sitting still and not talking for over an hour while the adults talk about incredibly boring things. You need to give them tasks and assignments that they can do. I have watched children, though, with proper training and praise, do amazingly well at the whole process of being more adult than the adults!

Practice

One of the most helpful and overlooked training technique for misdeeds is making the child do it right three to five times in a row. I have found this technique to be so helpful and clarifying for children. They really do need to practice doing something right so that they can get praise for it. This is using the rod (action) in one of the most helpful ways. It is causing the child to repeatedly do what you want them to do in the correct way. This is so much better than just telling. Sometimes a parent can see that the child does not really understand what the parent is asking for because they cannot perform the behavior even in practice. Practice the right behavior until they can do it flawlessly. Then congratulate them for learning this new behavior.

I can remember one time when my children were fighting to get into the house through the garage door and they slammed into the door and then pushed each other out of the way to get in. I raised my voice, and said, "Oh, that is no way to treat that door. Come back here and show me that you know how to go through the door with proper honor to the door and each other." I made them walk up to the door, open it slowly, and then enter one at a time. Then I had them come back and practice doing that five times. It was wonderful and they learned to treat each other and the door properly.

I found there are endless applications of the Practice method of child training as long as you realize the highest priority is training your children, not just getting to the next activity. So many of us have crammed our schedules so full we don't have time to do the essential training. Build into your schedule the time needed for having them practice getting into and out of the car five times. Going into the school five times. Going doing the aisle at the super market and getting a certain item five different times so they reinforce how to do it properly.

It will save you time and sanity in the long run.

Restraint

There are times when a child might hurt themselves if they were to dash out in to traffic or touch a hot stove or break sharp objects that could fall on them, and so forth. In these kinds of situations where a child could hurt themselves or others by their behaviors, it may be appropriate to restrain the child for a period of time until they have restored order to their actions.

Corporal Punishment

While this is a controversial practice, there are times of direct defiance and rebellion where some parents feel corporal punishment may be needed to sufficiently emphasize that the behavior just performed cannot and will not be tolerated. Care must be taken to ensure that the use of corporal punishment will not result in permanent injury. It is also important to note that the amount of corporal punishment should not exceed the level of open love and affection for the child. Some think it is naïve to believe that every child will respond to discussions and time-outs. There are times when a child basically says to their parents "make me!" It is at those times when corporal punishment may be appropriate.

One can definitely say that at those times of open defiance, it is time for parental action of some kind to correct the child. We have tried to outline many various ways for a parent to take action. There are times when talking is not enough. It is true that many have landed upon corporal punishment as the only type of parental action, which is clearly not the case. One should not take any corrective action out of anger or with the desire or intent to harm the child. When anger and/or harm is injected into corrective action, the lesson is lost on the child. The point of correction is to change the child's behavior the next time, not to instill fear, shame, or reactive anger in the child.

Creative Action to Remind

This is the creative action that causes your children to remember to make a different choice the next time. One of my daughters wanted a dog, and I did not think she was responsible at the time, so I had her walk an invisible dog every day for three weeks, feed an invisible dog for three weeks, and pick up the poop from an invisible dog for three weeks to prove to me she was ready for the responsibility of owning a dog. It took three tries over three years before my daughter completed the task and convinced me she was responsible enough to own a dog.

One time, one of my girls really threw a wrench in our family's plans because of a behavior issue she allowed to get out of control. I remember talking with her about how much her irresponsibility had completely changed the family's plans. So, I made and had her wear a necklace of two or three wrenches for an hour to help her realize that she had thrown a wrench in our family plans by her behavior.

Isolation

Our world has gone overboard on using time-outs for children who misbehave, but there are times when isolation (time-outs) is an appropriate way to change behavior in the child. Isolation is not the panacea that many people think it is, but it can be an effective tool for training. For some children, being forced out of the social gathering is the best way to help them grow, but for introverts, isolating them almost rewards them. Realize that training must bring about change in that child, not just be convenient for the parents. I can remember having one of my children sit by me while her sister got to go out and play in the play structure; it really made an impression on her that she should not behave in the way she had been behaving.

Rewards for Right Behavior

Some children respond best when they gain something for the desired behavior. It could be a treat or an item they've been wanting, but it should bring out the right behavior. This technique is used often in the learning of a new behavior. I have found Dr. Sal Severe's material in his book *How to Behave So Your Children Will, Too!* to be exceptional in seeing ways to reward children for positive behavior. His idea of "never give away the ice cream" has significant merit as long as it is not pushed too far.[9]

I used many of these ideas and specific rewards that were special to my children to motivate them to keep trying or to overcome the obstacles that at the time discouraged them. Dr. Severe has been a school psychologist for twenty-plus years and has collected a number of good ideas and practical advice for working with children in a school setting. Many of these ideas can translate to the family well.

Here is a modified list of fun activities and incentives that are sure to motivate your children:

Use the computer/device	Posters
Watching a movie together	Science kits

A special day with a parent	Working on models, building kits
Surprises	Board games/puzzles
Amusement parks	Magic tricks
Back rubs	Museums
Thank you notes in the lunch box	Making money
Thank you notes through the mail	Painting/drawing/supplies
Having lunch at school	Playing outside/Playing catch
Books/Reading a story	Sporting events
Baseball cards	Kite flying
Going for a walk/Going on a family bike ride	Going swimming, fishing/skating, bowling
Going for a drive	Playing miniature golf
Going on a mystery ride	Going to the movies
New clothes	Going to the zoo, park, museum, library
Watching television together	Going out to eat
Watching television alone	Allowing child to choose the restaurant
Renting a movie	Flying a remote-control plane
Playing video games together	Directing a remote-control car or boat
Teach the parent how to play a favorite game	Bubble baths/toys in tub
Using your phone or device	Brushing hair
Making popcorn	Helping prepare a meal/dessert
Staying up late on weekends	Helping mom or dad with projects
Spending time at a friend's house	Treats/Ice cream
Spending the night at a friend's house	Stickers/sticker books/happy faces
Having a friend come to the house	Stars/points on a chart
Having a slumber party	Money/allowance/savings account
Making a blanket tent	Mystery jar with awards inside
Camp-out in the backyard	Activities with friends/Going to the Mall/Shopping
Singing songs/Playing music	Having a pizza delivered
Going to a relative's house	Computer time/On-line account

The Six R's of Wise Parenting: Responsibility

Working on project with the parent	New clothes
Working on a project alone	Starting a business
Working on a project with a friend	Cosmetics/Hair Styled
Getting a pet	Doing work for money
Having a friend over for lunch/dinner	Having a weekly goal
Choosing an activity for the family	Projects/hobby supplies
Going out with a friend for lunch/dinner	Concerts
Working on cars/Using tools	Cooking
Time alone/Being allowed to do things alone/Choice time	Decorating their room
Staying up later than younger siblings	Pick their own time to do chores
Music or video game time	Going on a business trip with parent
School materials	Joining an organization with a parent
Go out for ice cream	Getting to participate in an older type activity
Special trips with school, church, clubs	Making a trophy for someone else
Dances/Parties/Evening events/Dating	Making a trophy for themselves
Getting their own phone	Learning a skill with a parent
Sporting events	Listening to a lecture or celebrity with a parent
Playing cards	Extended Curfew

Removal of Privileges

Some children are very motivated to change when certain, specific privileges are threatened. They so value those privileges, such as their phone, TV, friends, and youth group that they are willing to act differently so those privileges can continue. Again, let me remind you this is not about punishing your children; it is about *changing their behavior*. It does not matter if you want to take away privileges because you are so mad. It only matters whether this will bring about a new set of behaviors in your children.

Work

There are times when a child's attitude is out of sorts and/or they are rebellious; they need to work it out. In these cases, a slow and mindless task can help them work through the issues. I have known parents who have told their children, "Your attitude is not right; I think you need some time to change it, so I want you to vacuum the whole house." Other chores like this could be sweeping out the garage; cleaning the tiles in the shower; shoveling the snow in the driveway; dusting the furniture in the house. The key idea is that when their attitude is different and the chore is done, it is over. If their attitude is the same (surly and rebellious), then the chores keep coming.

Exercise

There are times when even chores and work will not change the child's attitude and orientation. In these instances, some parents have used push-ups, pull-ups, sit-ups, and jumping jacks, even running laps! The child needs to work out this level of aggression and rebellion. They need to realize that this kind of attitude and behavior will not be tolerated. This is essentially a military-training technique without the drill instructor shouting insulting remarks at them. It is an effective method for helping your children realize that they can change their attitude and behavior any time they want to, and if they don't, it will be unpleasant but not harmful for them.

See appendix 4 for an overview of the Actions (Rod) consequence options. I have found it helpful to have this on the refrigerator so that you can have ideas of what to do in the spur of the moment when raising your kids.

TEACHING FORGIVENESS: A MUST IN THE TRAINING PROCESS

One of the most important lessons about teaching responsibility is forgiveness. No one is perfect, neither your children or you. I wanted my children to hear me apologize to them when I had been wrong and I wanted them to apologize to me when they had been wrong. One must know how to admit mistakes, receive forgiveness, and give forgiveness. It is very important to realize that training is a process that can be emotional, spiritual, mental, and physical. When children or parents have not been responsible in what they say, do, or emote, then there needs to be a repair to the relationship. I have found these steps to be very helpful in repairing a relationship and also teaching your children how to repair relationships in other parts of their life.

We knew in our parents' generation this would not have been done. We really wanted to make sure that our kids knew when we made a mistake. Having clear and open communication and peace has shaped our current relationships in to what they are today—loving, open, and close.

Be gentle in spirit. No one wants to repair a relationship with a person who is arrogant, demanding, critical, or irritating. If you have messed up in some way, there must be a gentleness and a humility in order to begin the repair.

Seek education. This is where a person who wants to repair a relationship asks the person who is or may be offended how they have been offended. This is a crucial step in that the offender needs to hear from the offended one what was done to damage the relationship. This part of the repair process takes the most time.

Admit you were wrong. Once the person has shared how you offended them, then there is a need for an admission of guilt (unless it is a true misunderstanding). It is helpful for the offended person to hear that the offender was wrong. Say, "I was wrong, when I did…"

Ask for forgiveness. This is where the offender asks for the offended person to forgive them. "Will you forgive me?" Wait for a yes or no.

Develop a repentance plan. This is where a particular offense has been committed over and over again or it was so egregious that the person needs some proof that the offender will not do it again. It is kind of like a "what do I get to do to you if you do this again" clause. When the level of pain or gain is great enough, then the offended person can embrace the desire for a restored relationship.

Test for openness. Are they open to you in terms of other conversation topics? Are they open to you hugging or touching them? We asked our children to hug us after each time we had to work through a discipline issue. This allowed us to gauge the level of openness of the relationship and the thoroughness of the repentance.

Conclusion

Enjoy the training process. The eighteen years will go by incredibly fast. Every few years, the challenges will change but the goal stays the same. *My child must realize they are responsible for their actions, their words, their bodies, their attitudes, their emotions.* They may not have caused all the things that happened, but they are responsible for their choices.

As you think about training your child, a key question to ask is,

"What will make my child realize their responsibility for what they did and make for the right choice the next time?"

Another question to ask yourself is,

"Is what I am doing causing a change in the behavior of my child?"

If the answer is no, then no matter how much you want what you are doing to work, it is clearly not working with that child, so change to a different way of interacting with that child about their choices. Do not keep doing the same corrections or punishments if it is not bringing about better behavior. Realize that what you are doing is not working and jump to a different method.

I have tried to cover in a dozen pages or so the practical ways to love your children into adulthood. It is all about love. You want the best for them. You want them to succeed beyond you when they enter the world and start to make their mark. This means that they must learn how to be responsible. They must understand the power of choice and how to wield its power. They must understand that everything they say, think, do, emote, and base their actions upon is a choice. God wants to partner with them to be moral, loving agents of His, but He will not make the choices for them. They must choose, and the results will either fall on them or bless them. It is a wonderful thing to see your children succeed. It is a dark thing to see your children struggle. What you do in this area of responsibility will determine a lot about whether you rejoice with your children or weep for them.

QUESTIONS TO ASK AT THE WEEKLY STAFF MEETING:

- Are our kids growing responsible in the control of the body, mouth, helpfulness, and so forth?
- Where is each child being irresponsible?
- Is there an irresponsibility that is the greatest issue in their life this week?
- What choices is this child consistently making positively? How do we praise this?
- What choices is this child consistently making negatively? How to we change this?

Final Thoughts

Having children has been one of the great joys of my life. I was excited when each of our daughters were born. I was excited during each phase of the parenting process, even though sometimes I was completely terrified. My wife and I did not do a perfect job, no parent does. But we did the best we could with the training we had received. All of my children are adults now living successful lives. I love them so very much. It has gone by incredibly fast and I am filled with wonderful memories. I regret some things, and I have apologized to each of my children for ways I was not everything I should have been. I have told each of my children numerous times how I love them and that I am proud of them.

If I can do this parenting thing, you can do this parenting thing. I encourage you to work hard at developing a real relationship with your children; never miss an opportunity to let them know how much you respect them; give them all the resources you can for them to fly higher than you ever did; help them know the rules of life—its expectations and boundaries; build into their life the routines that will allow them to be successful; open their eyes to the responsibility they have for their choices—they can make their life great or not so great by their choices.

Let me end where I began. Use the weekly staff meeting to discuss, strategize, pray, and implement your parenting plan. You and your spouse are the experts on parenting your children. What you do and how you do it can be so right for your child. The village you collect around you for this family-raising adventure will be crucial. This whole trip through *Wise Parenting: Creating the*

WISE PARENTING: Creating the Joy of Family

Joy of Family is designed around the six elements that need to be constantly injected into your family. Discussing them weekly with your spouse and your village will work wonders through the eighteen to twenty-five years you are raising your children (and they are raising you).

Think of these elements as the agenda each week for the children portion of your staff meeting. Yes, there will be things that you didn't anticipate or don't know how to deal with, but someone does or someone can help you. Your children are excited to be raised by you in an environment of relationship, respect, resources, rules, routines, and responsibility. You will not be perfect, but you can have a joyful family full of love and respect. It doesn't take lots of money or wisdom; it takes a willingness to engage in this supremely important task of raising the next generation.

A SIMPLE WEEKLY PLAN
(have this discussion)

	MOM	DAD	CHILD 1	CHILD 2	CHILD 3
Relationship (LOVE)					
Respect (VALUE)					
Resources (TOOLS)					
Rules (INSTRUCTION)					
Routines (TRAINING)					
Responsibility (CORRECTION)					

Take an hour every week to discuss these 6 topics.
What 1 area do you want to focus on per family member?

Final Thoughts

Just having the six categories with their sub-ideas is very helpful to guide a discussion with your partner. (See appendix 6—Six R's of Wise Parenting Table.) You probably won't go over every issue every week, but it is significant to see the options and ideas every week. On most weeks, my wife and I just had these ideas listed on a piece of paper. This was to remind us of each category and to discuss them all even though we were coming into the meeting wanting to talk about one or two specific things.

Remember that all of these details are just a way to remind you of the various things to talk about and be aware of during the course of your children's growing up. Sometimes this list can be overwhelming as it is really a listing of all the things that will be covered over the eighteen years of their life with you. I understand. Just keep at it patiently and consistently.

Enjoy your children.

Enjoy the process.

Allow God to guide you as you bring them up in the nurture and admonition of the Lord.

notes

1. "The Significance of a Father's Influence," Focus on the Family, 2011; https://www.focusonthefamily.com/family-qa/the-significance-of-a-fathers-influence/; and "Statistics on Fatherless Children in America," Wayne Parker, May 24, 2019, https://www.liveabout.com/fatherless-children-in-america-statistics-1270392.

2. Dr. Ruby Payne, *A Framework for Understanding Poverty, 4th Edition* (Highlands, TX: aHa! Process, Inc., 2005), 7f.

3. Erik Rees, foreword by Rick Warren, *S.H.A.P.E.: Finding and Fulfilling Your Unique Purpose for Life* (Grand Rapids: Zondervan, 2006).

4. Buckingham, Marcus, Clifton, Donald, *Now Discover Your Strengths* (New York: The Free Press, 2001), 50–52.

5. Center on Addiction's National Survey: Teen Insights into Drugs, Alcohol, and Nicotine, June 2019. https://www.centeronaddiction.org/addiction-research/reports/teen-insights-drugs-alcohol-and-nicotine-national-survey-adolescent

6. Keller, Helen, *The Story of My Life* (New York: Dover Publications, 1996).

7. Canfield, Jack, *The Success Principles: How to Get from Where You Are to Where You Want to Be* (New York: Harper Collins, 2015), 141–42.

8. Dr. William Glasser, *Positive Addiction* (New York: Harper & Row, Publishers, Inc., 1976), and *Choice Theory* (New York: Harper Collins

Publisher, 1999).

9. Dr. Sal Severe, *How to Behave So Your Children Will, Too!* (Tempe: Greentree Publishing, 2000).

10. Dr. Ruby Payne, *A Framework for Understanding Poverty, 4th Edition* (Highlands, TX: aHa! Process, Inc., 2005), 7f.

appendix
1

Personality Tests and Other Resources

Male vs. Female differences

There are a number of online resources that report the differences between the genders in terms of verified tests. One of the first books to release much of these results was *Why Gender Matters* by Leonard Sax.

Myers–Briggs

There are a number of professional and amateur versions of the Myers–Briggs test. Numerous books have also sought to add clarity and expertise to the observations of these temperament differences. Some of the best know have been *Please Understand Me* by Kiersey and Bates.

DISC Test/Ancient Temperaments

The DISC test has been used in work place settings for years and has offered a quick guide to understanding people's natural impulses in various settings. One of the most complete approaches to this personality assessment is *The Everything DISC Manual* by Mark Scullard and Dabney Baum.

Love Languages

The discovery that people give and receive love in five major ways has been revolutionary for relationships. The truth that people have one major and one minor channel to give and receive love in the most impacting and resonating ways has repaired and revitalized many relationships. Dr. Gary Chapman has written extensively in this area: *The Five Love Languages* is the most popular book on this topic.

Spiritual Gifts

The truth that God has given Christians special abilities to use His power for the benefit of other believers and the world has transformed people, churches, and communities. When people can allow God to flow through them in the ways that He desires, great things happen. There are many books on spiritual gifts from different theological perspectives. Find a book on this subject from your theological perspective, take the test, and let God flow through you to others.

Natural Abilities

The Johnson O'Connor research laboratory has been studying natural abilities and how to test for them for almost a hundred years now. These types of actual tests have helped thousands of people realize hidden talents and find joy in doing what they were made to do. Margret Broadly has written the most complete summary book about this vital work in her book *Your Natural Gifts*. It is an older book but it gives the best overview. Please contact the Johnson O'Connor Research Laboratory online and in major cities around the globe. www.sf@jocrf.org.

Strengths Finders

Donald Clifton and many others in the Gallup organization have created a wonderful test for determining what a person's recurring pattern of excellence are. This has become an industry standard for many organizations. "What are your top five strengths?" is a good question in many interviews. There are now many books that detail the work of the strength finders themselves, but the original *Strength Finders* book is still the one to start with.

Eye-Memory Patterns

Psychology has suggested that eye movements are an indicator of what is going on in the brain since William James in the 1800s. This idea has been fleshed out in the last fifty years with some interesting and intriguing results. It is extensively developed in Neuro Linguistic Programming literature. The connection between eye movements and the way a person processes information and prefers to process information is very helpful for relationships and personal development. Much has been written and discussed online and through various forums on this subject. It can be very helpful to understand what the eyes are saying as people seek to build healthy relationships.

Socio-Economic Hidden Rules and Background

Much work has been done in the area of class distinctions and the hidden rules by Dr. Payne in her book *A Framework for Understanding Poverty*.[10] Her work has been ground-breaking and can help unlock the grip of poverty and victimization that has landed on many families. The idea that there are hidden rules that operate in the various classes of society has been eye-opening for many educators, officials, churches, and individuals. The understanding of these hidden rules has allowed significant personal development and organizational effectiveness.

Hidden rules are everywhere in life, and make it work. These are the cultural, class, subcultural, governmental, and financial rules that either pave the way to success or throw obstacles in our way. To the child, the world presents itself as a simple set of rules that everyone should follow. As the child grows, it becomes clear that the world is not always fair or easily understood. There are hidden rules that only some people know about and follow. The ones who do are typically more successful in life.

The advanced or "hidden" rules supersede the simple rules. This is true in finances, social settings, class distinctions, cultural and subcultural environments, vocational assignments and promotion, and even spiritual settings. If parents don't help their children see the basic rules as well as the more advanced ones, the child will not likely make as much progress as they could, or they may conclude they are cursed or victims.

Knowing the hidden rules is one of those areas our children would find helpful in understanding what they are naturally directed towards, much like understanding temperaments, love languages, and natural abilities. They feel impulses toward certain ideas and values that will be different in other people.

I have found this understanding to create many "a-ha moments" for individuals and families when they understand the values and rules communicated via the class-structure they were raised in.

Family of Origin and Cultural Programming

One of the key insights that people must glean is that much of who they are was influenced or even programmed by the actions and decisions of their parents and culture. The idea of tracing out a genogram to understand what happened before you has been revolutionary for many people. Look at how your parents and culture handles various tasks, difficulties, and interactions allows a person to evaluate why they just instinctively do many things in their life. If these patterns can be examined, they can be evaluated for their help or harm to your life and relationships. One of the key Christian books that has helped explore this crucial area is Pete Scazzero's book, *Emotionally Healthy Spirituality*.

appendix 2

The following is the actual placemat we placed under my children's plates each evening.

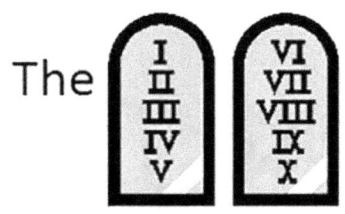

The Commandments

You shall have no other god's before Me

You shall not make for yourselves any graven images

You shall not take the Name of the Lord your God in vain

Remember the Sabbath day to keep it holy.

Honor your Father and your Mother

You shall not murder

You shall not commit adultery

You shall not steal

You shall not bear false witness against your neighbor

You shall not covet anything that belongs to your neighbor

WISE PARENTING: Creating the Joy of Family

Here are other placemats we used on occasion to teach other biblical concepts and to reinforce the key scriptures into their hearts.

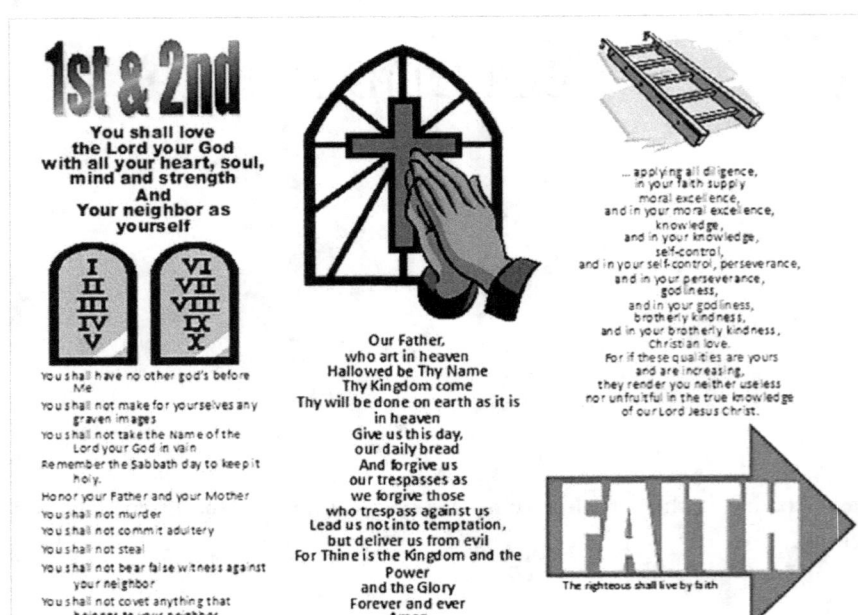

1st & 2nd

You shall love the Lord your God with all your heart, soul, mind and strength
And
Your neighbor as yourself

I, II, III, IV, V, VI, VII, VIII, IX, X

You shall have no other god's before Me
You shall not make for yourselves any graven images
You shall not take the Name of the Lord your God in vain
Remember the Sabbath day to keep it holy.
Honor your Father and your Mother
You shall not murder
You shall not commit adultery
You shall not steal
You shall not bear false witness against your neighbor
You shall not covet anything that belongs to your neighbor.

Our Father,
who art in heaven
Hallowed be Thy Name
Thy Kingdom come
Thy will be done on earth as it is in heaven
Give us this day,
our daily bread
And forgive us
our trespasses as
we forgive those
who trespass against us
Lead us not into temptation,
but deliver us from evil
For Thine is the Kingdom and the Power
and the Glory
Forever and ever
Amen

...applying all diligence,
in your faith supply
moral excellence,
and in your moral excellence,
knowledge,
and in your knowledge,
self-control,
and in your self-control, perseverance,
and in your perseverance,
godliness,
and in your godliness,
brotherly kindness,
and in your brotherly kindness,
Christian love.
For if these qualities are yours
and are increasing,
they render you neither useless
nor unfruitful in the true knowledge
of our Lord Jesus Christ.

FAITH
The righteous shall live by faith

The fruit of the Spirit is
**Love
Joy
Peace
Patience
Kindness
Goodness
Meekness
Faithfulness
and
Self-Control**
against such things
there is no law

Be-attitudes

Blessed are the poor in spirit, for theirs is the kingdom of heaven.

Blessed are those who mourn, for they shall be comforted.

Blessed are the meek, for they shall inherit the earth.

Blessed are those who hunger and thirst for righteousness, for they shall be satisfied.

Blessed are the merciful, for they shall receive mercy.

Blessed are the pure in heart, for they shall see God.

Blessed are the peacemakers, for they shall be called sons of God.

Blessed are those who have been persecuted for the sake of righteousness, for theirs is the kingdom of heaven.

Blessed are you when people insult you and persecute you, and falsely say all kinds of evil against you because of Me. "Rejoice and be glad, for your reward in heaven is great; for in the same way they persecuted the prophets who were before you.

The Apostle's Creed

I believe in God,
the Father Almighty,
the Creator of heaven and earth,
and in Jesus Christ,
His only Son, our Lord:
Who was conceived
of the Holy Spirit,
born of the Virgin Mary,
suffered under Pontius Pilate,
was crucified, died,
and was buried.
He descended into hell.
The third day He arose again
from the dead.
He ascended into heaven
and sits at the right hand of God the
Father Almighty,
from whence He shall come to judge
the living and the dead.
I believe in the Holy Spirit,
the holy universal church,
the communion of saints,
the forgiveness of sins,
the resurrection of the body,
and life everlasting.
Amen.

God	Self	Marriage/Dating	Family	Work	Church	Money	Society	Friends	Enemies

appendix 3

Lesson 1: Explain the Box

The Box

You live in the box made of my rules for your conduct.

Lesson 2: Anger and Consequences

Stay in the Box

Stay inside of the commands & desires of your parents, and you will be in the joy of your mother and father.

Lesson 3: The Box Can Change to Be Bigger

Lesson 4: The Box Can Change to Be Smaller

Lesson 5: Living within God's Box

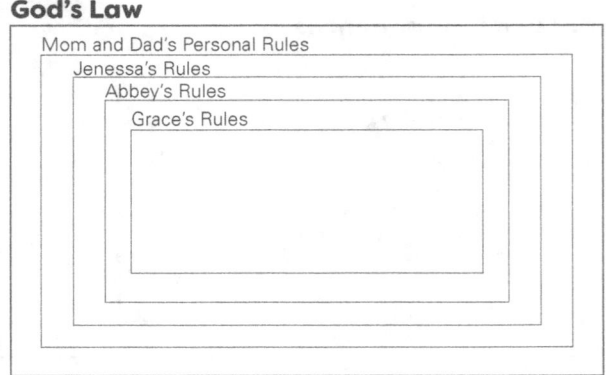

Appendix 4

CONSEQUENCES: WORDS

WORDS (REPROOF)

Reset Expectations (before each thing, new routines)

Verbal Repetition (tell me...)
Praise, Verbal, Written, Tanglible

Intense Emotional Reminder
Kneel, Eye-to-eye, "I feel..."

Earned Responsibilitiy
(negotiated actions for rewards)

Deal with Guilt

Five Questions:
What did you do?
Was it the right thing?
What could you have done?
What has to be done to make you remember?
What will you do next time?

Contract
(I agree to do this, you agree to do that)

Process Pain and Learn to Forgive

Repair Broken Relationships

Consequences: Actions

ACTIONS (THE ROD)

Demonstrate the Desired Behavior

Practice
(do it 5 times)

Isolation
Time out, Grounding, Go to room

Chastisement
(for open rebellion or immediate danger)

Creative to Remind
(necklace of wrenches, invisible dog example)

Rewards
(new behaviors)

Remove Privileges
(Xbox, driving, sports, phone, activity)

Restraint
(physical, mental, police)

Work to Blow off Steam
(pull weeds, vacuum, dust, etc.)

Exercise
(sit-ups, pull-ups, push-ups, run, jumping jacks)

Create Your Village
Mentors / Role Models
Grandparents / Relatives
Family Friends
Instructors / Tutors / Coaches
Leaders
Babysitters
Other Parents

Appendix 5

WISE PARENTING SLIDES

• There are 8 resources that your children need from you to become independent successful adults.

1. <u>Wisdom</u>, Knowledge Understanding & Prudence Resources Pro 8:12-14
2. <u>Financial</u> Resources
3. Mental Resources
4. <u>Emotional</u> Resources
5. Spiritual Resources
6. Physical Resources
7. Support <u>Systems</u> Resources
8. <u>Role Models</u> Resources

- State the Expectation
- Explain the Expectation
- Demonstrate the Expectation
- Practice the Expectation

- <u>Re-state</u> the expectation
- <u>Re-explain</u> the expectation
- <u>Re-demonstrate</u> the expectation
- <u>Re-practice</u> the expectation

With <u>Teens</u>

- <u>Ask</u> them about the objective / expectation
- <u>Discuss</u> the Expectation
- <u>Agree</u> on the Expectation
- <u>Demonstrate</u> the Expectation
- <u>Practice</u> the Expectation

- Re-Ask about the expectation
- Re-discuss the expectation
- Re-demonstrate the expectation
- Re-practice the expectation

Many problems in a family happen because some one does not <u>know</u> or is not <u>following</u> the routine that is in someone else's head

Eating Out Routines	Bedtime Routines	Driving Routines
Store Routines	Personal Hygiene Routines	Money Routines
Guest Routines	Midweek Routines	Homework Routines
Waking Up Routines	Vacation and/or Holiday Routines	Romance Routines
Morning Routines	Sunday Routines	Friend Routines
Dinner Time Routines	Elders Routines	Planning Routines
Evening Routines	Family Devotions Routines	Chores Routines

Appendix 6

Six R's of Wise Parenting Table

	Dad	Mom	Child 1	Child 2	Child 3
Relationship • Work with: • Talk with: • Play with: • Parents • Mentors/Role models/ Authorities • Friends • Romance • God • Siblings • Music/Movies/TV • Magazine/Computer/ Internet/Social Media/ Video Games/Books					
Respect • Value • Importance • Compliments • Titles • Authorities • Things					
Resources • Finances • Emotional/Mental • Spiritual • Physical • Support Systems • Role models/Mentors					
Rules • Set expectations • Explain/Demonstrate • Practice • Boundaries/No guard rails					
Routines • Explain/Demonstrate • Practice for everything					

Responsibility
• Training needed
• Positive choices
• Consequences:
  - Reproof (Words)
  - Rod (Actions)					

About Gil & Dana Stieglitz

Dr. Gil Stieglitz is a prolific author, engaging speaker, and insightful pastor who has spent thousands of hours helping, coaching, and strengthening marriages. Gil has written over 25 books on marriage, parenting, soul development, and spiritual warfare, including top-seller *Becoming a Godly Husband, Marital Intelligence, God's Radical Plan for Wives,* and his newest book, *Building a Ridiculously Great Marriage.* He speaks to thousands of people each year about the wonders of God's principles. Gil now serves as Discipleship Pastor at Bayside Church, a dynamic multi-site church near Sacramento, CA, and is the founder of Principles to Live By, a nonprofit organization that helps people connect to God's principles in everyday life.

Dana Stieglitz has a Doctor of Nursing Practice from Samuel Merritt University. She works as Nurse Practitioner in a Physical Medicine and Rehabilitation practice located in Sacramento, CA. Dana also co-authored *Becoming a Godly Wife* and *God's Radical Plan for Wives.* She enjoys training Pilates Instructors, travel, food tours, and hanging out with her girls.

Together, Gil and Dana have raised three beautiful young women who exemplify the Six R's in their own unique ways. For more information and to check out their other books and resources, visit www.ptlb.com or Amazon.com.

About Principles To Live By

Principles to Live By is a 501(c)3 organization that equips and empowers people, pastors, and churches. Our biblical resources, coaches, counselors, and teachers magnify God and ignite hope for better relationships, healthier Christians, thriving churches, and vibrant communities. PTLB hopes to reach hundreds and thousands of people with God's principles for transformational change. For more information and to donate, visit www.ptlb.com.

More PTLB Resources

Books (www.Amazon.com)

Becoming a Godly Husband

Becoming Courageous

Breakfast with Solomon, Volumes 1–3

Breaking Satanic Bondage

Building a Ridiculously Great Marriage (2019)

Deep Happiness: Eight Secrets

Delighting in God

Delighting in Jesus

Developing a Christian Worldview

Getting God to Talk Back: Secrets of the Lord's Prayer

God's Radical Plan for Wives

God's Radical Plan for Wives Companion Bible Study by Jennifer Edwards

Going Deep in Prayer: Forty Days of In-Depth Prayer

Keeping Visitors

Leading a Thriving Ministry

Marital Intelligence: There Are Only Five Problems in Marriage (Reprinted 2019, BMH Books)

Mission Possible: Winning the Battle over Temptation

Proverbs: Devotional Commentary, Volumes 1–2

Satan and the Origin of Evil

Secrets of God's Armor

Spiritual Disciplines of a C.H.R.I.S.T.I.A.N.

The Gift of Seeing Angels and Demons: A Handbook for Discerners of Spirits by Susan Merritt

The Keys to Grapeness—Growing a Spirit-led Life

The Schemes of Satan

They Laughed When I Wrote Another Book about Prayer, Then They Read It

Touching the Face of God: Forty Days of Adoring God

Uniquely You: A Faith-Driven Journey to Your True Identity and Water Walking, Giant-Slaying, History-Making Destiny by Jenny Williamson

Weapons of Righteousness Study Guides

Why There Has to Be a Hell

Audio Books (Amazon.com)

Becoming a Godly Husband (to come)

Building a Ridiculously Great Marriage

Wise Parenting: Creating the Joy of Family (to come)

Online Video Courses (www.Udemy.com)

Becoming a Godly Husband

Mission Possible: Winning the Battle over Temptation

The Keys to Grapeness—Growing a Spirit-led Life

Spiritual Disciplines of a C.H.R.I.S.T.I.A.N. (coming soon)

Audio Files (www.ptlb.com)

Becoming a Godly Husband

Becoming a Godly Parent

Biblical Meditation: Keys of Transformation

Deep Happiness: Eight Secrets

Everyday Spiritual Warfare Series

God's Guide to Handling Money

Intensive Spiritual Warfare Series

Marital Intelligence: Battling for Your Marriage

Raising Your Leadership Level: Double Your Impact

Spiritual War Surrounding Money

Spiritual Warfare: Using the Weapons of God to Win Spiritual Battles

The Four Keys to a Great Family

The Ten Commandments

Weapons of Righteousness Series

www.PTLB.com

www.ingramcontent.com/pod-product-compliance
Lightning Source LLC
LaVergne TN
LVHW051604070426
835507LV00021B/2751